MW01528376

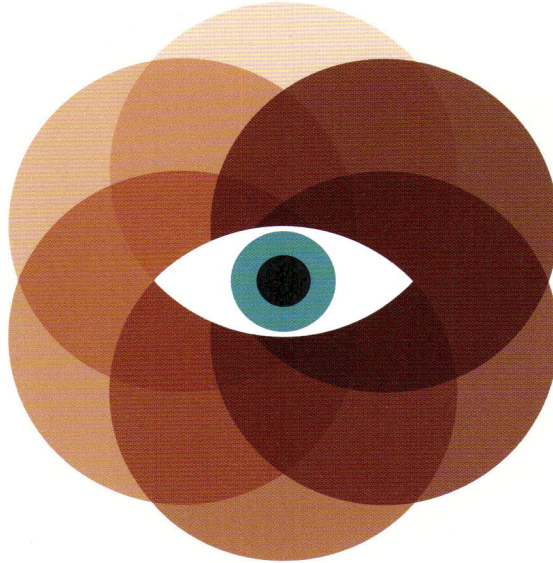

THE PORN PHENOMENON

The Impact of Pornography in the Digital Age

Research commissioned by:
Josh McDowell Ministry
(a Cru Ministry)

Research conducted by:
Barna Group, Ventura, California

The Porn Phenomenon © 2016 by Josh McDowell Ministry. All rights reserved.

ISBN 978-0-9965843-6-4

All information contained in this document is copyrighted by Josh McDowell Ministry, a Cru Ministry and shall remain the property of Josh McDowell Ministry. U.S. and international copyright laws protect the contents of this document in their entirety. Any reproduction, modification, distribution, transmission, publication, translation, display, hosting or sale of all or any portion of the contents of this document is strictly prohibited without written permission of an authorized representative of Josh McDowell Ministry.

The information contained in this report is true and accurate to the best knowledge of the researchers and the copyright holder. It is provided without warranty of any kind: express, implied or otherwise. In no event shall Josh McDowell Ministry, Barna Group or their employees be liable for any special, incidental, indirect or consequential damages of any kind, or any damages whatsoever resulting from the use of this information, whether or not users have been advised of the possibility of damage, or on any theory of liability, arising out of or in connection with the use of this information.

Unless otherwise indicated, Scripture quotations are from the *New Living Translation* copyright ©1996, 2004, 2007, 2013 by Tyndale House Foundation. Used by permission of Tyndale House Publishers Inc., Carol Stream, Illinois 60188. All rights reserved.

CONTENTS

PREFACE
by Josh McDowell

Practically every pastor, youth worker, Christian educator and parent says they want to pass on their faith, morals and values to the next generation. I have spent the vast majority of my life trying to help in that mission.

About six years ago, I began to sense something was seriously wrong. I couldn't quite put my finger on it. Whatever it was, it was negatively affecting the receptivity of young people to the biblical faith that parents and churches so desperately want to pass on.

After a lot of questions and investigation, I concluded that young people are being overwhelmed by Internet pornography. The easy access our kids have to pornography is distorting their views of morality and the Christian faith.

While there was good secondary research on the issue, I became convinced that a study among pastors, youth pastors and churched youth and adults was necessary in order to understand the contours of the crisis. Without primary research, I feared it would be difficult to awaken the Church to the emergency.

I consulted key pastors and Christian leaders. Chuck Swindoll encouraged the research initiative and told me he believes pornography is the greatest cancer in the Church today. Dr. James Dobson was also supportive but warned there would be resistance because church leaders caught in the grip of porn are burdened with shame and an incredible fear of being discovered.

Nevertheless, I pressed forward.

Barna Group, under the leadership of David Kinnaman, agreed to take on the challenge. In the end, *The Porn Phenomenon* became one of the most comprehensive studies Barna has conducted to date. The goal was to assess the extent to which pornography has permeated Christian families, the Church and our society at large, and to determine its impact.

I've often said that a problem well defined is a problem half solved. This study defines the problem—but it also goes well beyond that. Be prepared for an eye opener!

The Porn Phenomenon is a wakeup call. When 54 percent of Christian young adults ages 18 to 24 seek out porn at least occasionally, and when two out of three youth pastors and more than half of senior pastors say porn is a current or past struggle, we have a genuine crisis on our hands. Porn is undermining God's truth in the lives of young people and eroding the credibility of the Church.

Pornography is not new. However, the digital tools that deliver and propagate it today *are* new, and they have fundamentally changed the landscape. But not even the ubiquity and easy access of smartphone and tablet apps will be able to compete with the coming advancements in virtual reality (VR) technology. VR systems such as Oculus Rift, Samsung Gear VR and HoloLens immerse the user visually and sonically in a virtual world. In the near future, all three systems will have add-on devices that bring other parts of the user's body into the virtual space—meaning a user won't just see and hear but also touch and feel virtual objects and people as if they were real.

This technology has promising implications for manufacturing design, the medical field, other sciences and the arts. But it is not difficult to imagine the devastating capacity of VR devices to lure an entire generation deeper into a virtual world of pornography, turning what is already a crisis into an epidemic of addiction.

We must act quickly and create better ways of talking about the problem of porn. This study is a good start. We need a culture among church leaders and parents that is more conducive to transparency and emotional safety, where Christians of all ages can admit their struggles. We need to extend more grace and offer greater hope: People *can* be restored by God's grace through the body of Christ.

PORN IS UNDERMINING GOD'S TRUTH IN THE LIVES OF YOUNG PEOPLE AND ERODING THE CREDIBILITY OF THE CHURCH

In some places, the Christian community is beginning to take positive steps. Pastors, youth workers and parents are coming out of the shadows to sound the alarm. Individuals and groups are creating resources that offer help and healing. For example, I partner with a group called Covenant Eyes (www.covenanteyes.com) to promote Internet accountability and filtering services for individuals, families and churches.

We can combat the porn phenomenon. More importantly, we can win the battle—if we act now. The apostle Paul's challenge to the first-century church is as relevant today as then:

> Use every piece of God's armor to resist the enemy in the time of evil, so that after the battle you will be standing firm. Stand your ground, putting on the sturdy belt of truth and the body armor of God's righteousness. For shoes, put on the peace that comes from the Good News, so that you will be fully prepared (Eph. 6:13–15, NLT).

WE CAN COMBAT THE PORN PHENOMENON. MORE IMPORTANTLY, WE CAN WIN THE BATTLE

INTRODUCTION
Why the Church Can No Longer Ignore Porn

Thirty years ago, pornography arrived in the mail wrapped in discreet black plastic. It was checked out for rental from the "special section" behind a curtain in the neighborhood video store. It was purchased from magazine racks raised out of children's reach (unless the kids were tall, or enterprising, or both). It was commonly understood that some men looked at porn— but as a general rule they weren't proud of it, and most wouldn't have dreamed of bragging about it.

Times have changed.

Today, porn slips invited or not onto every screen with an Internet connection. For that matter, much of it *originates* in regular households with a wireless signal: 50 percent of young women ages 13 to 24 who use porn say they have sent a nude image via text, email or smartphone app.

Attitudes about porn have changed, too.

Three-quarters of young men 13 to 24 talk with their friends about porn at least occasionally. And nine out of 10 of them say that *how* they talk about porn is encouraging, accepting or neutral. It is commonly understood that most of their friends regularly use porn—and as a general rule they are ho-hum about it.

This is not the case in the Christian community. Certainly, a significant number of practicing Christians (and of pastors) use porn. But many of these folks feel acute guilt and shame when they do, and most say they have no one they trust who can help them stop.

These twin realities—the ubiquity of porn today and the unwillingness or inability of local Christian communities to talk about it—have precipitated a crisis the Church can no longer afford to ignore.

In early 2015 Josh McDowell and his team visited the Barna offices because they wanted to help the Church start talking about porn. In order to do that in a responsible way, they believed, we needed reliable data about people's use of and attitudes toward pornography.

The Porn Phenomenon is the culmination of a multiphase data-gathering project conducted and analyzed by Barna researchers on behalf of Josh McDowell Ministry. We surveyed nearly 3,000 U.S. teens, adults and Protestant youth and senior pastors about their perceptions of pornography, their use of pornography, how they feel about their use of pornography and much more.

This monograph presents a summary of the data gathered by Barna, as well as secondary research and cultural observations that help make sense of the numbers. In addition, we interviewed a handful of knowledgeable people to get their perspectives and insights (these are included as Q&As throughout the book) and invited Bob Harper, a local pastor here in Ventura, California, to reflect on the questions ministry leaders should be asking themselves in response to these findings. (You'll find his questions in the margins to amplify your reading.) In the appendix, there are fact sheets for a number of key population segments, such as teens ages 13 to 17, practicing Christian men, youth pastors and so on. At a glance, you can see each group's views of porn, how frequently and the reasons they use it, and how they tend to feel about their porn use.

With Josh and his team, Barna's hope is that this data will catalyze a conversation in the Church about how best to respond to the porn phenomenon.

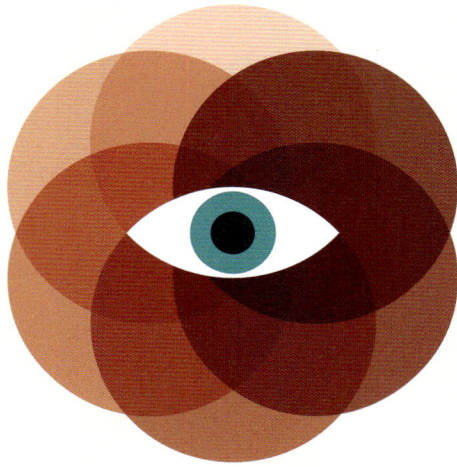

WHAT WE'RE TALKING ABOUT WHEN WE TALK ABOUT PORN

Pornography is notoriously difficult to define and often very subjective. It was important then, at the very outset of the study, for Barna Group to determine how people define pornography. To understand, in other words, what people are talking about when they talk about porn.

FORM VS. FUNCTION

Defining pornography takes two distinctions: both form and function. For many people the content (the form) is less of a measure than the intention of the producer or of the viewer (the function).

FORM

81%

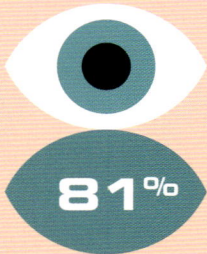

An image of sexual intercourse

57%

A fully nude image that is sexually arousing

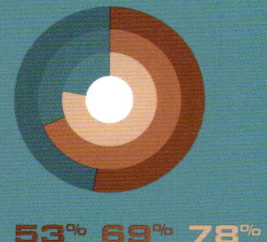

62%

An image of a sexual act that is not intercourse

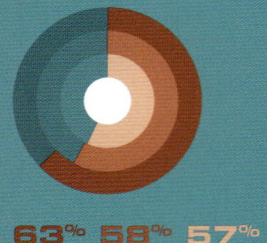

VS

FUNCTION

85%

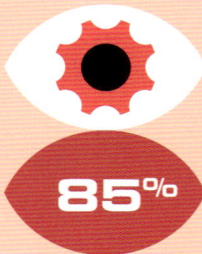

Sex scenes that make up most or all of a video with very little story

70%

If you watch / listen to / read it specifically for the purpose of sexual arousal

60%

If you masturbate while viewing / reading

*asked only among those ages 13-24

TEENAGERS ARE MORE LIKELY TO CALL SOME- THING PORN

Which of the following do you definitely consider to be porn?

An image of sexual intercourse

79% 87% 90%

A fully nude image that is sexually arousing

53% 69% 78%

An image of a sexual act that is not intercourse

63% 58% 57%

Legend

- Adults
- Young adults
- Teens

A fully nude image

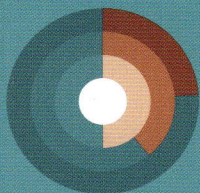

24% 39% 50%

A partially nude image

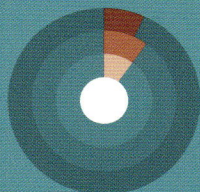

7% 10% 10%

EXCEPT WHEN IT COMES TO SEXTING

Chatting or texting about sexual acts with someone you do not know personally

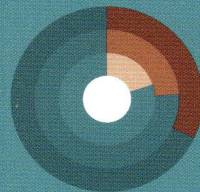

32% 24% 20%

5 SIGNS IT'S PORN

The following are the top five indicators for people that something has "crossed the line" into porn.

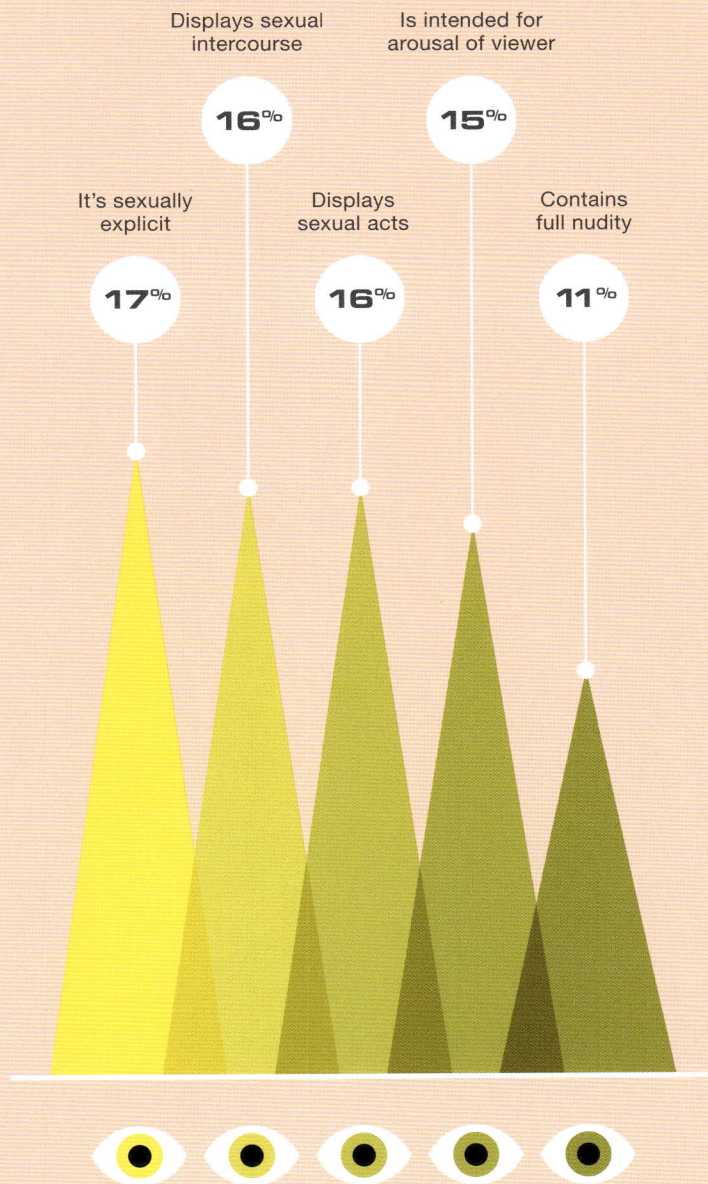

Displays sexual intercourse
16%

Is intended for arousal of viewer
15%

It's sexually explicit
17%

Displays sexual acts
16%

Contains full nudity
11%

an open-end question asked among Americans 13+

LOOK WHO'S TALKING ABOUT PORN

36%

20%

MEN TALK ABOUT PORN MORE THAN WOMEN

Talk about porn with friends at least occasionally

- Males, 13-24
- Females, 13-24

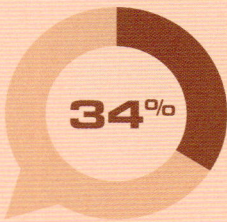

34%

18%

YOUNG ADULTS TALK ABOUT PORN MORE THAN TEENS

Talk about porn with friends at least occaionally

- Young adults
- Teens

TEENS AND YOUNG ADULTS HAVE A PRETTY CAVALIER ATTITUDE WHEN TALKING ABOUT PORN WITH FRIENDS

Most teens and young adults are either encouraging, accepting or neutral when they talk about porn with their friends

- Teens
- Young adults

90%

13% Encouraging: We talk about porn in a positive, lighthearted way

40% Accepting: It's just assumed we all look at porn sometimes

37% Neutral: We don't really discuss the morality of it

96%

17% Encouraging: We talk about porn in a positive, lighthearted way

43% Accepting: It's just assumed we all look at porn sometimes

36% Neutral: We don't really discuss the morality of it

Only one in 10 teens and one in 20 young adults says their friends think viewing pornography is a bad thing.

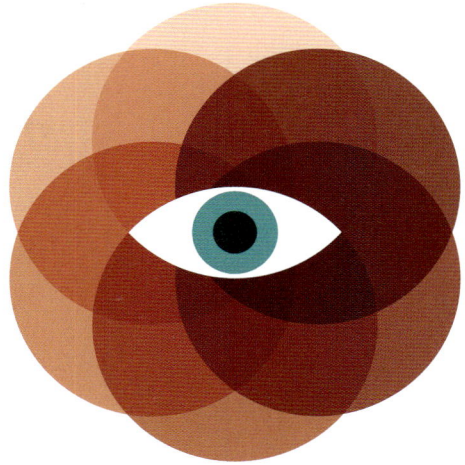

1.

THE LANDSCAPE OF PORN

"I know it when I see it." So said Supreme Court Justice Potter Stewart when he was asked to define pornography.

His oft-quoted statement demonstrates a perennial problem: It is notoriously difficult to define pornography. What counts as sexually explicit material is both highly subjective and highly contested—especially considering recent and rapid shifts both in pornography's form (that is, the media used to create and deliver it) and its function (people's reasons for producing or viewing it).

The word "pornography" is a combination of two Greek words: *pornē*, meaning "prostitutes," and *graphein*, "to write about." In ancient times, pornography was not images but words.

A modern cultural understanding of pornography started with words, too. It began to emerge when the first erotic novels were published in Victorian-era England.[1] These books spun tales of sexual exploits intended to sexually arouse the reader and, shortly after they were published, pornography was criminalized by the British Parliament in the Obscene Publications Act of 1857.[2] According to the law, content alone does not

According to the New Testament, sin is both an act (see Rom. 3:23) and an intention (see Matt. 5:28). Jesus favors addressing the intention as the key to stopping the act (see Matt. 15:16–19). Is this our pattern, as well? What can we do to help people deal with their intention toward porn and, as a consequence, strengthen their ability to resist the act?

BOB HARPER
Pastor of Ventura Vineyard

The ministry application questions found throughout this monograph were contributed by Bob Harper, who pastors the Ventura Vineyard, a church he planted more than 15 years ago. He earned an MA in theology from Fuller Seminary and now coaches and mentors church planters and emerging leaders in the U.S., Eastern Europe and Asia. Bob has been married for 35 years to Margie, with whom he has three grown children and one grandchild.

make pornography of words or images. An equally important element is the *function* of the content—that is, the purpose intended by the creator, adopted by the user, or both.

This definition created two required components of pornography: *form* and *function*. The 1857 law thus codified the first culturalized understanding of pornography. And though form has evolved significantly since the nineteenth century, the notion of function remains important for today's understanding of what counts as pornography.

Why does this matter? Because if you're like many leaders, your first impulse is to be concerned with content (form) rather than function. But a person's intentions toward sexually explicit content are a more pressing matter. Certainly, blocking access to content can be helpful as a first step for a person who wants to be free from porn use. But, as we will hear from our expert contributors, the heart—the desires and longings that lie deep within—must be transformed if the person is going to experience true freedom.

WHAT IS PORN?

How do Americans define pornography? While nearly everyone agrees that "an image of sexual intercourse" is definitely porn, the issue of function seems to be at the center of most people's thinking. If you use it for masturbation or personal arousal, it's porn. Simple as that.

Most of us have probably been to an art museum or taken an art history class in which we saw a fully nude statue or painting. You probably didn't consider that pornography, and most Americans agree with you. Less than one-quarter of adults over age 25 (24%) consider a fully nude image to be objectively pornographic.

But if it that fully nude image is sexually arousing, that's a different story. Half of adults over age 25 (53%) say that "a fully nude image that is sexually arousing" is definitely pornography. It is the second-highest defining factor in the younger age groups, with nearly seven in 10 young adults (68%) and eight in 10 teenagers (78%) agreeing.

When asked what is "definitely porn," teenagers and young adults are more likely than older adults to consider any of the options to be pornography. This may come as a surprise. One might assume that, having grown up in a hypersexualized culture where nude images and sexual situations are part of everyday life, younger Americans might have become sexually desensitized. But it seems such desensitization takes time—curiosity and the "forbidden" nature of sex may play a role in teens and young adults feeling as if more content is risqué.

IF YOU'RE LIKE MANY LEADERS, YOUR FIRST IMPULSE IS TO BE CONCERNED WITH CONTENT (FORM) RATHER THAN FUNCTION

WHAT IS *DEFINITELY* PORN?
% "definitely" among U.S. teens, young adults and adults 25+

- an image of sexual intercourse
- a fully nude image that is sexually arousing
- an image of a sexual act that is not intercourse
- a fully nude image
- a partially nude image

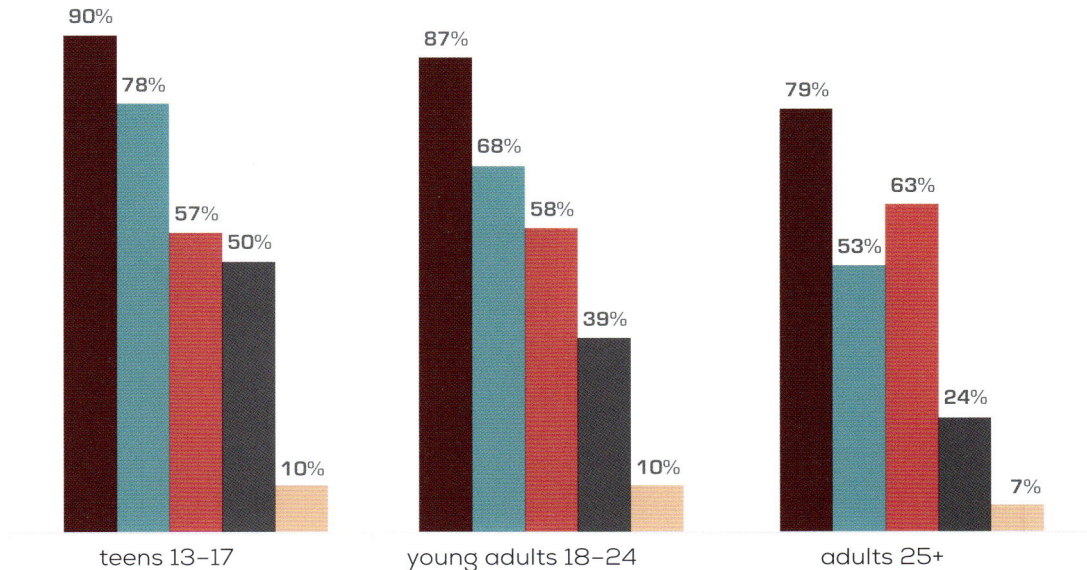

teens 13–17
- 90%
- 78%
- 57%
- 50%
- 10%

young adults 18–24
- 87%
- 68%
- 58%
- 39%
- 10%

adults 25+
- 79%
- 53%
- 63%
- 24%
- 7%

FOR TEENS AND YOUNG ADULTS, THE PURPOSE BEHIND VIEWING AN IMAGE— ITS FUNCTION FOR THE USER— IS CRITICAL

For these teens and young adults, the purpose behind viewing an image—its function *for the user*—is critical to determine whether something qualifies as porn. When these groups are asked what kind of viewing situation classifies images or words as porn, seven out of 10 say the key element is watching, listening or reading *for the purpose of sexual arousal*. Again, function is key.

WHAT MAKES SOMETHING PORN?

% among U.S. teens and young adults who actively seek out porn

if you watch / listen / read it specifically for the purpose of sexual arousal	70%
if you masturbate while viewing / reading	60%
if you pay for an image that is sexual in nature	53%
if you interact with someone or something sexual in nature	48%
if you get sexual images for free	40%
if the image is NOT personal—of someone you don't know	39%
if you watch / listen with a romantic partner	30%
if you watch / listen / read it alone	27%
if the image is personal—of someone you know	25%
if the nude person is yourself	23%
if you watch / listen / read with friends	17%

70% of teens and young adults say arousal is what makes something porn

For many people who use porn, it's not just the user's intent that defines something as pornographic, but also the producer's intent. More than eight out of 10 adults 25 and older indicate an image is porn if it is comprised of "sex scenes that make up most or all of a video, with very little story" (84%); two-thirds consider a "still picture of sexual acts" to be pornography (66%); and six in 10 consider "close-up still pictures of genitals" to be porn (61%). Teens and young adults report similar views, but are again somewhat more likely to put many of the options in the porn category.

IMAGES & ACTIVITIES THAT ARE *DEFINITELY* PORN
% among U.S. teens, young adults and adults 25+ who actively seek out porn

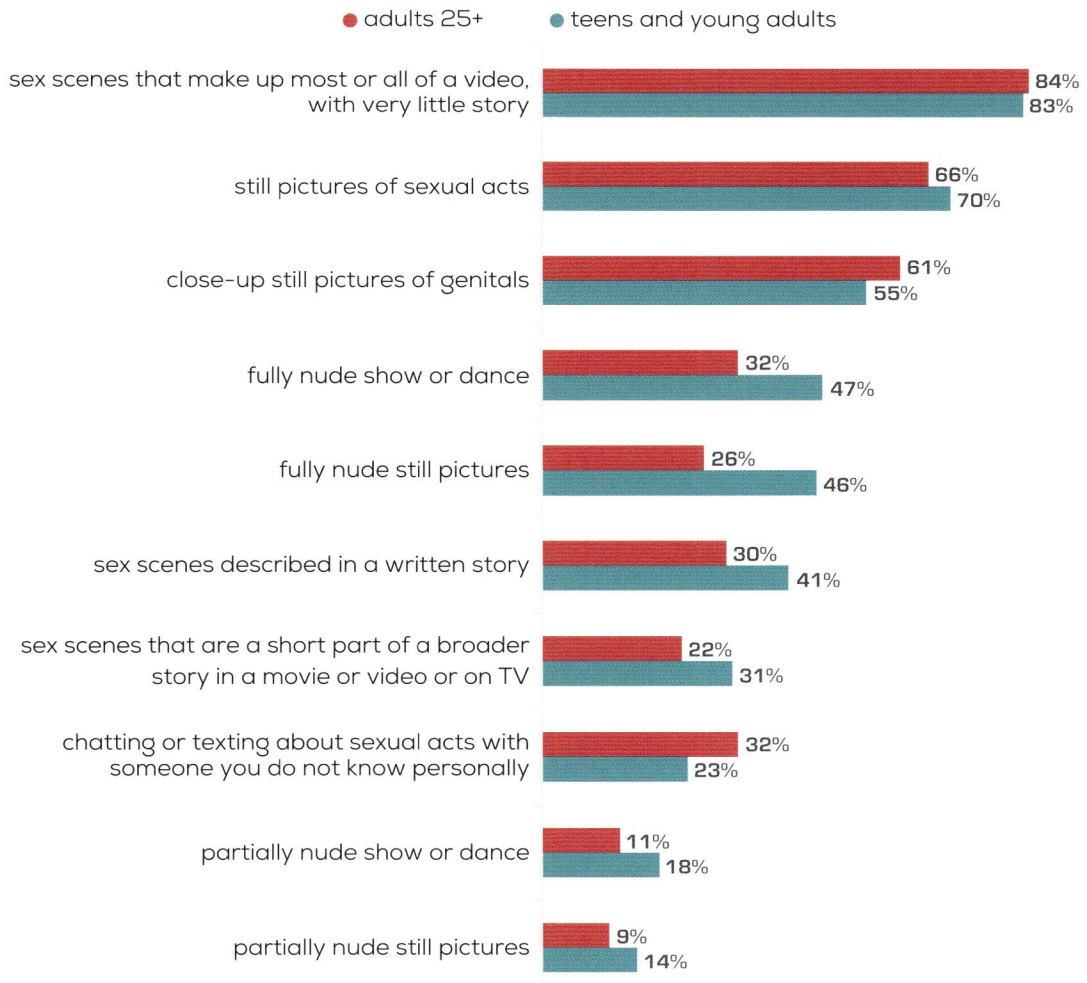

● adults 25+   ● teens and young adults

	adults 25+	teens and young adults
sex scenes that make up most or all of a video, with very little story	84%	83%
still pictures of sexual acts	66%	70%
close-up still pictures of genitals	61%	55%
fully nude show or dance	32%	47%
fully nude still pictures	26%	46%
sex scenes described in a written story	30%	41%
sex scenes that are a short part of a broader story in a movie or video or on TV	22%	31%
chatting or texting about sexual acts with someone you do not know personally	32%	23%
partially nude show or dance	11%	18%
partially nude still pictures	9%	14%

The context of a sex scene also matters a great deal to people's perceptions. A lack of narrative seems to indicate to most teens and adults that the primary purpose of the scene is to arouse the viewer—and that the scene is therefore porn. On the other hand, "sex scenes that are a short part of a broader story" are considered pornographic by just two in five adults (22%) and three in 10 teens and young adults (31%). If a sex scene is integral to a story, most Americans do not consider it pornography.

The genesis of pornography—the written word—still counts as porn for some Americans. Three in 10 adults (30%) and four in 10 teens and young adults (41%) consider sex scenes described in a written story to definitely be porn. The massive popularity of the *50 Shades of Grey* novels lends credibility to this idea.

THE EVOLUTION OF PORN

Gradually through the twentieth century, courts abandoned the criminalization and censorship of pornography and, in the absence of a clear legal definition, cultural definitions grew increasingly hazy. Moreover, the invention of photography, magazines, film and video, mobile phones and the Internet created new media (form) through which pornography could be created and consumed.

As pornography has become normalized and entered the cultural mainstream, it's also become more explicit, violent and racist. As early as the 1980s, scholars such as Andrea Dworkin condemned pornography as a tool of male dominance that eroticizes the humiliation and abuse of women.[3] True as it was 30 years ago, pornography has hardened even since then. Porn today is more hardcore, is more explicitly degrading and dehumanizing, and places an even greater focus on aggressive sexual activity.[4]

In her book *Pornland*, Gail Dines argues that the increasing prevalence of porn means men are becoming desensitized to it. In order to experience arousal, therefore, many seek out ever harsher,

AS PORNOGRAPHY HAS BECOME NORMALIZED AND ENTERED THE CULTURAL MAINSTREAM, IT'S ALSO BECOME MORE EXPLICIT, VIOLENT AND RACIST

more violent and more degrading images.[5] Also, the increasing amount of free online porn has led commercial pornographers to produce more extreme content to compete.[6] So demand for hard-core content is both real (from consumers) and manufactured (by producers).

According to famous porn star and adult film director James Deen, racism is also rampant in the industry, both on camera and behind the scenes.[7] "Interracial" is a popular subgenre of porn, and these scenes often trade on "the racist idea that white women are violating themselves by having sex with black men."[8]

Scholar Robert Jensen claims these realities present us with a moral paradox: What does it say about a "civilized" society that accepts and promotes a mass media genre that is overtly cruel to women and explicitly racist?[9]

Compared to 150 years ago, porn's twenty-first–century iteration is more complex. For one thing, ease of access has never been greater—a fact mostly attributable to the explosive growth and widespread dissemination of new communication technologies during the past two decades. The level of privacy the Internet affords—particularly when the intention is to masturbate—significantly reduces the psychological barriers to entry. Where once you had to walk into a store and show your face in order to access pornography, anyone can find porn today from the privacy of their bedroom with just a few clicks.

Use of pornography has become culturally embedded alongside the Internet. Estimates of pornographic websites range from 4 percent[10] to 12 percent[11] of all sites on the Web and, according to some claims, up to 40 million Americans are regular visitors to porn sites.[12] In 2015, there were more than two billion online searches for pornography.[13] The proliferation of high-speed Internet and Internet-enabled devices has fundamentally altered the ways people view and interact with pornography.[14] These technological realities have "indiscriminately allowed people of all ages to encounter and consume sexually explicit content."[15]

Robert Jensen asks a question that exposes the gap between intention and act on a cultural level: "What does it say about a 'civilized' society that accepts and promotes a mass media genre that is overtly cruel to women and explicitly racist?" Rather than addressing the wider culture with biblical injunctions against sexual immorality (a tactic that doesn't seem to be working very well), what would it look like for the Church to speak prophetically to the culture about its own hypocrisy?

The Web has by far eclipsed all other avenues for accessing pornography. Among those who report having viewed porn, seven out of 10 adults (71%) and 85 percent of teens and young adults have done so using online videos. Six in 10 adults (59%) and two-thirds of teens and young adults (65%) view porn *mostly* online. Magazines and video rentals are passé.

Smartphones offer new and dynamic means of accessing and distributing pornography. Apps and text are an increasingly popular option, especially among teens and young adults. While just 12 percent of adults 25 and older view porn *mostly* on their phone, teens and young adults are three times more likely to do so (38%). (Read more about this phenomenon in the special report "Porn 2.0" on page 28.).

The proliferation of digital tools has blurred the lines between porn producers, distributors and consumers. Barriers to entry and transaction costs—such as the affordability of video equipment, for example, or the abundance of user-friendly online platforms and services—have fallen and "enabled consumers to produce and distribute their own pornography."[16]

The historically *passive consumer* has evolved into today's *active producer*—a result not only of changing technology, but also of shifting social norms of self-expression.[17] Blogging, online dating, text messaging and social media have become vehicles of "oversharing" in the Internet age, a phenomenon that muddles the boundary between public and private life and has had a profound impact on the shape of pornography today.[18] In addition, smartphones, texting and apps such as Snapchat, Instagram and others have enabled what we call "Porn 2.0."

THE PROLIFERATION OF DIGITAL TOOLS HAS BLURRED THE LINES BETWEEN PORN PRODUCERS, DISTRIBUTORS AND CONSUMERS

TALKING ABOUT PORN

As any parent or youth pastor can tell you, the teen and young-adult years are characterized by sexual discovery and identity

THE WAYS PEOPLE VIEW PORN, BY AGE

% among U.S. teens, young adults and adults 25+
who actively seek out porn

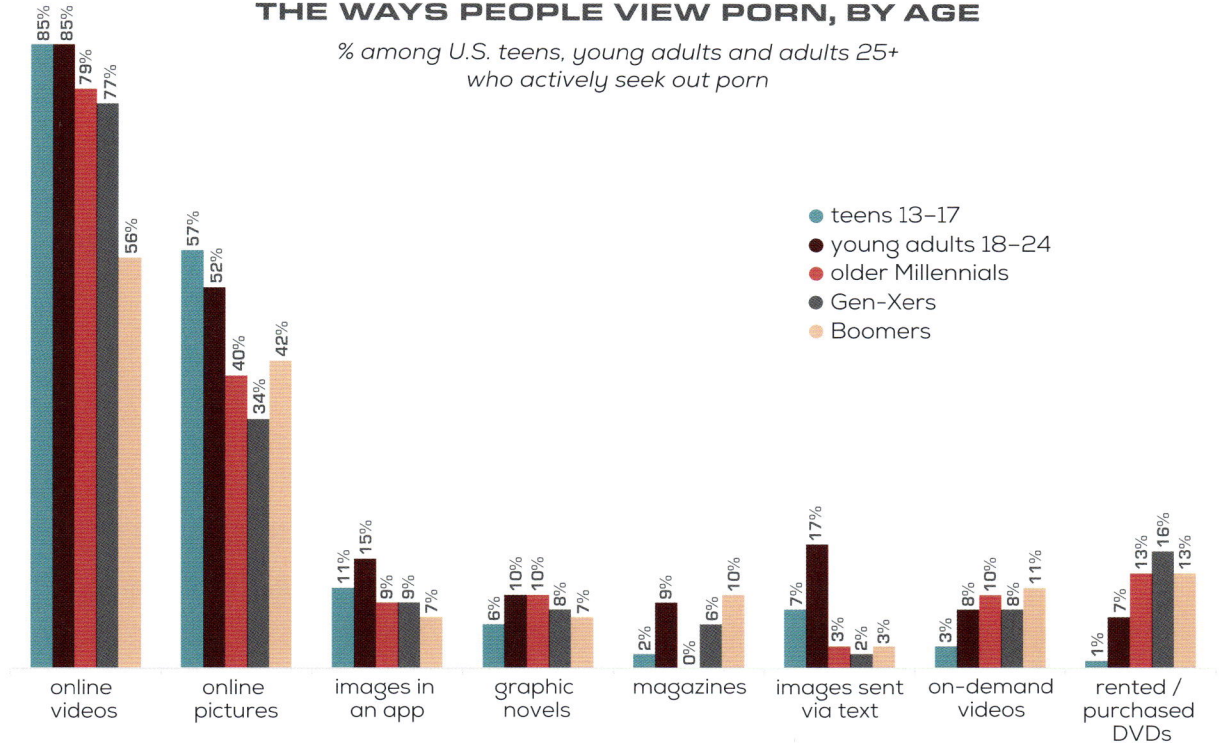

- teens 13–17
- young adults 18–24
- older Millennials
- Gen-Xers
- Boomers

	teens 13–17	young adults 18–24	older Millennials	Gen-Xers	Boomers
online videos	85%	85%	79%	77%	56%
online pictures	57%	52%	40%	34%	42%
images in an app	11%	15%	9%	9%	7%
graphic novels	6%	10%	10%	8%	7%
magazines	2%	9%	0%	6%	10%
images sent via text	7%	17%	3%	2%	3%
on-demand videos	3%	8%	10%	8%	11%
rented / purchased DVDs	1%	7%	13%	16%	13%

formation—and much of that work is done in the company of peers. It is therefore unsurprising to find that more than one-quarter of 13- to 24-year-olds talk to their friends about porn, either often or occasionally (28%). Young adults (34%) talk about porn more often than their teenage counterparts (18%). Heading off to college and breaking away from parental supervision may create conditions for greater freedom to discuss and explore sexual topics. (The fact that half of young adults estimate that "all" or "most" of their friends regularly look at porn, compared to only one-third of teens, supports this case.) Peer evaluation, guidance and approval are a more prominent part of life in young adulthood. As such, discussions about porn may more easily become part of everyday interactions.

49%
of young adults say all or most of their friends use porn regularly

HOW OFTEN DO YOU TALK ABOUT PORN WITH YOUR FRIENDS?

% among U.S. teens and young adults

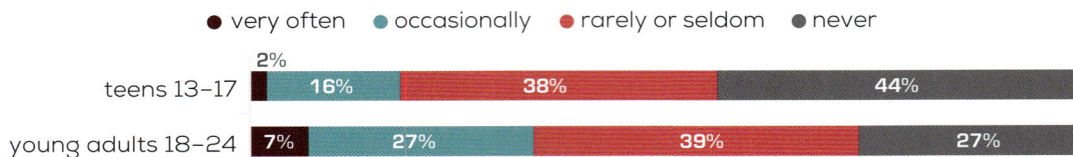

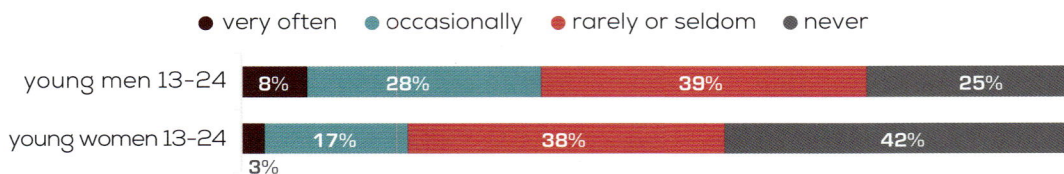

● very often ● occasionally ● rarely or seldom ● never

	very often	occasionally	rarely or seldom	never
teens 13–17	2%	16%	38%	44%
young adults 18–24	7%	27%	39%	27%

HOW OFTEN DO YOU TALK ABOUT PORN WITH YOUR FRIENDS?

% among U.S. teens and young adults

● very often ● occasionally ● rarely or seldom ● never

	very often	occasionally	rarely or seldom	never
young men 13–24	8%	28%	39%	25%
young women 13–24	3%	17%	38%	42%

Women who have participated in widely viewed sex tapes are now rich celebrities, admired by teens and young women as people to emulate. And, according to this research, "The historically passive consumer is turning into an active consumer." Along with more holistic and biblical teaching on sex, how can the Church help young people become more critical consumers of culture?

Predictably, young men (36%) report talking about porn with their friends more often than young women (20%). This may be because men look at porn more often than women—at least, that seems to be the general assumption among teens and young adults. (It's also true.) Twenty-two percent say men view porn most often; 42 percent say "mostly men and a few women" consume pornography; and about one-third say porn consumption is split evenly between the sexes (33%).

Among those who talk with friends often, occasionally or seldom about pornography, most do so in a way that is either accepting (42%) or neutral (36%). An additional 16 percent talk with their friends about porn in a positive or lighthearted way, with no one expressing shame for having viewed it. Teens and young adults generally assume that most people look at porn at least on occasion, and the morality of porn is rarely discussed or even considered. Just one in 10 teens and one in 20 young adults report talking with their friends about porn in a disapproving way.

THE WAY TEENS & YOUNG ADULTS TALK ABOUT PORN

% among U.S. teens and young adults who talk about porn with their friends

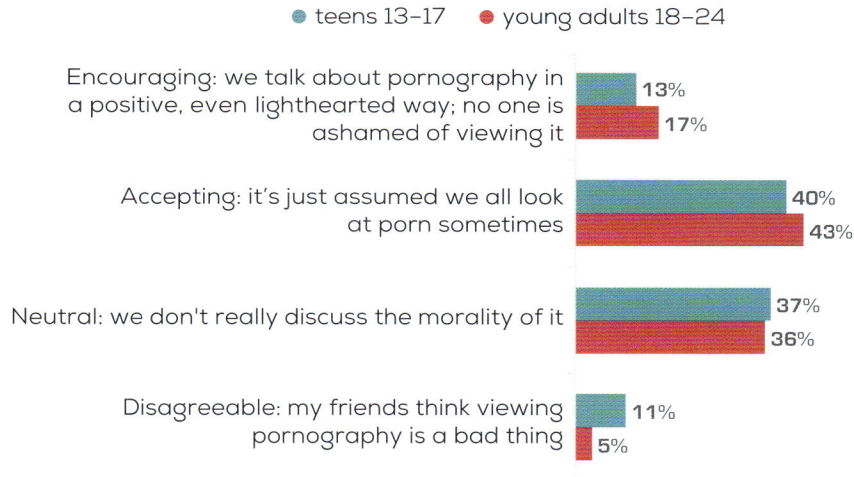

● teens 13–17   ● young adults 18–24

Encouraging: we talk about pornography in a positive, even lighthearted way; no one is ashamed of viewing it
- 13%
- 17%

Accepting: it's just assumed we all look at porn sometimes
- 40%
- 43%

Neutral: we don't really discuss the morality of it
- 37%
- 36%

Disagreeable: my friends think viewing pornography is a bad thing
- 11%
- 5%

These somewhat cavalier attitudes make sense when one considers young people's assessment of porn's prevalence among their friends. Half of young adults (49%) and one-third of teens (32%) say all or most of their friends regularly view porn.

In the next chapter, we'll find out if they're right.

HOW MANY OF MY FRIENDS REGULARLY VIEW PORN

% among U.S. teens and young adults

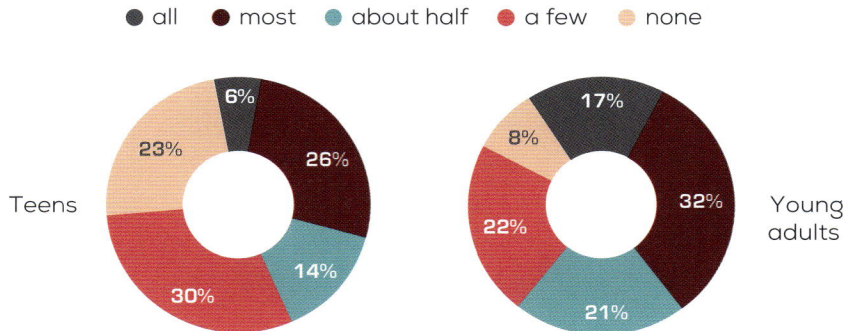

● all   ● most   ● about half   ● a few   ● none

Teens
- all 6%
- most 26%
- about half 14%
- a few 30%
- none 23%

Young adults
- all 17%
- most 32%
- about half 21%
- a few 22%
- none 8%

▶ **Q&A** WITH **JEFFERSON BETHKE**

JEFFERSON BETHKE
Speaker and author

Jeff lives in Maui with his wife, Alyssa, and daughter, Kinsley. He is the author of the books *Jesus > Religion* and *It's Not What You Think*. In addition to writing, Jeff makes YouTube videos and hosts a podcast with his wife. He has a yellow lab named Aslan and enjoys reading good books and drinking good coffee.

www.JeffBethke.com
@JeffersonBethke

Q: You've talked about today's teens and young adults being the most "exploited and exploitive" generation ever let loose on the world. How do you see porn contributing to their exploitation? What results do you think we'll see if the trend continues?

A: For starters, we are being exploited by advertisers and people behind the websites who make billions off our addiction, which in my opinion is immoral in itself (similar to drug dealers making money by supplying people with something that ruins their lives). But our generation is also exploiting each other all the way down the ranks through sexting, exchanging nude photos and perpetuating the culture and need that leads others to do things like trafficking and illegal exploitation.

Q: In 2015 you uploaded a video that draws a straight line between porn and human trafficking, pointing out the irony that Millennials fight sex trafficking more than any other generation—and they also consume more porn. Thinking about conversations you've had with porn users, does considering the possibility of exploitation and abuse seem to make a difference in their choice to continue?

A: It does seem to make a difference. One thing the Millennial generation hates is hypocrisy. And there isn't anything much more hypocritical than fighting trafficking while porn grows as one of the biggest consumer industries in the world. It's simple supply and demand. The demand that traffickers supply starts with pornography.

Q: Our culture's obsession with objectifying and using women's bodies is a theme that runs through your videos on sex and porn. Why do you think that's such an important message to focus on when you discourage porn use? And what do you think the Church can do in response?

A: I think the problem behind the problem to almost all brokenness in the world is commodification of another human. We use, abuse and exploit other humans for the thing we want—money, power, satisfaction, whatever. The minute a human becomes a stepping stone to something else, that's the minute you turn the most glorious thing in the world, another human, into a product or commodity. I think the problem of porn starts there. I read a quote somewhere that said something like, "Success happens when a guy looks away from porn not because of shame, but when he has such a high view of women that it's nearly impossible to get aroused from their exploitation."

Q: Looking at the Barna findings, what (if anything) stands out to you as encouraging, and why? What (if anything) do you find discouraging, and why?

A: One thing I found discouraging is that most people don't seem to realize porn is eroding the sacredness of sexuality and creating a low view of sex. But the encouraging thing is to see just how many people struggle with it. I think that information can be powerful for people because it seems to be a thing that thrives in darkness and isolation. But when other guys see they aren't alone, there is a lot of healing power.

SPECIAL REPORT
PORN 2.0

51% of teen and young adult women porn users have sent a nude image via text, email or app

The cavalier attitude of most teens and young adults toward porn, coupled with accessibility created by technology, is pushing pornography into a new era that is more social, interactive, dynamic and personal. The majority of teens and young adults (62%) report receiving a nude image from someone else via text, email, social media or app. Among those who have received a nude image, 58 percent say it was sent by their boyfriend or girlfriend and 21 percent say it was sent by a friend. More rarely the nude image was sent through a group of friends (3%).

TEENS & YOUNG ADULTS WHO HAVE *RECEIVED* NUDE IMAGES

% among U.S. teens and young adults who actively seek out porn

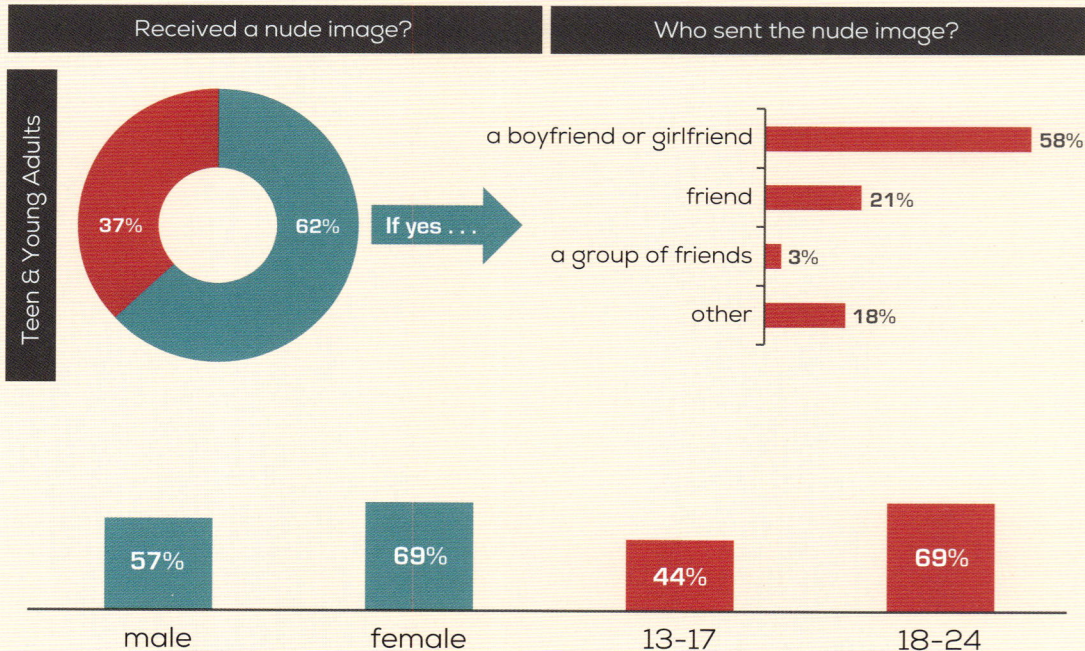

Received a nude image?	Who sent the nude image?

Teen & Young Adults

37% 62%

If yes . . .

- a boyfriend or girlfriend — 58%
- friend — 21%
- a group of friends — 3%
- other — 18%

male	female	13-17	18-24
57%	69%	44%	69%

Compared to the two-thirds who have received a nude image, just 40 percent of teens and young adults have *sent* such images to someone via text, email, social media or app. Because there are fewer senders than receivers, it is likely that senders tend to send images to more than one person. Senders most often send images to their boyfriend or girlfriend (75%), which may indicate that sexting is becoming an accepted practice of dating culture. It also may explain why young adults are more likely than teens to send and receive nude images: They have greater freedom to date around when they're not living at home.

Compared to men, women more often receive (69% vs. 57%) and send (51% vs. 33%) nude images via text, email, social media or app. The reasons for this gender disparity are unclear and more research is needed to explore the social pressures or lack of inhibition young women experience related to sexting.

TEENS & YOUNG ADULTS WHO HAVE *SENT* NUDE IMAGES

% among U.S. teens and young adults who actively seek out porn

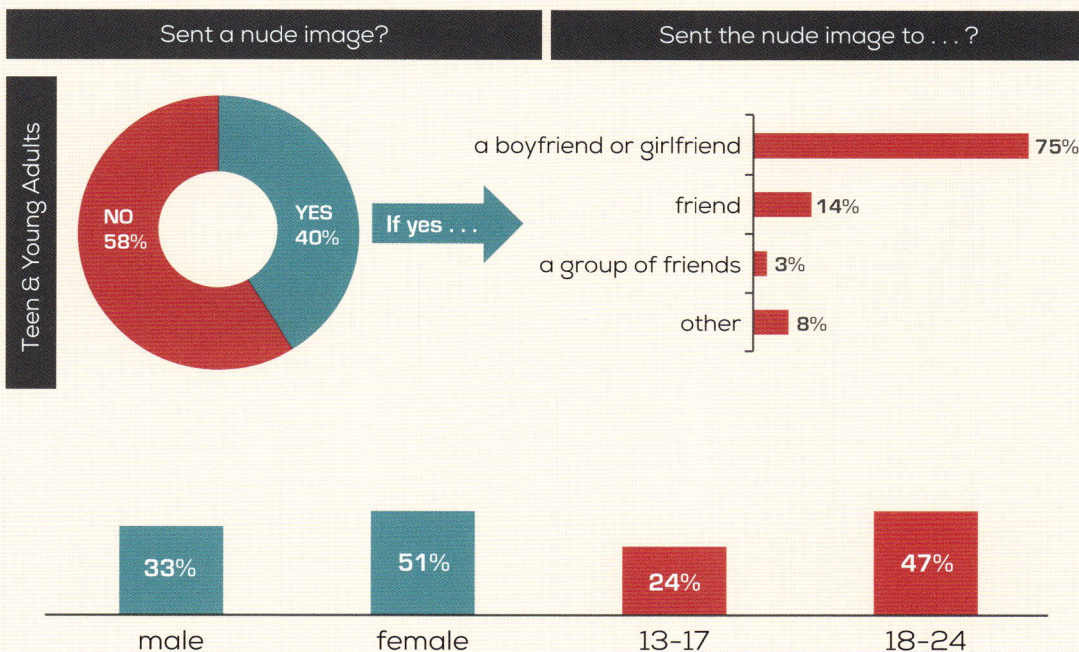

| Sent a nude image? | Sent the nude image to . . . ? |

Teen & Young Adults

NO 58%   YES 40%

If yes . . .

a boyfriend or girlfriend — 75%
friend — 14%
a group of friends — 3%
other — 8%

male	female	13-17	18-24
33%	51%	24%	47%

Digital cameras are now ubiquitous and are connected directly to the online universe; social networking sites allow for the exchange of these images; and the genre of "amateur," "reality," and "voyeur" porn has enticed many to utilize these technologies to broadcast themselves in what has become a frenzied, chaotic, and impossible-to-control pornographic landscape.[19]

Among teens and young adults, sexting and sharing explicit images through social media apps like Snapchat and Instagram have become commonplace. However, minors who send or receive sexual images often do not recognize the serious social, legal, emotional and psychological risks of doing so—particularly in cases where images are shared without consent.[20] In which case, things can go horribly wrong:

Jesse Logan, an eighteen-year-old high school senior from Ohio, sent a nude photo of herself to her boyfriend, who then made the decision to forward it to four other girls. The photo went viral, and Jesse was ostracized by her peers and quickly spun into an emotional depression. Taunted and labeled a "slut," a "whore," and a "porn queen," Jesse Logan hanged herself at her home a few months later.[21]

Another case demonstrates the complexities involved when the students are minors:

In the winter of 2010 in Lacey, Washington, a fourteen-year-old named Margarite took out her cell phone and snapped a full-length photo of herself, naked, in her bathroom mirror. She then sent the photo to a potential new boyfriend, Isaiah, at his suggestion. A few weeks later, Isaiah forwarded the photo to another eighth-grade girl, a former friend of Margarite's, who transmitted it (along with the text "Ho Alert!") to dozens of others on her cell phone contact list. Margarite became instantly (in)famous in her middle school; other kids began calling her a "slut" and a "whore," and she received sneers and ogles from peers she barely knew. Her friends were ostracized for associating with her. School officials soon discovered the situation, and the police were notified. Reaction was swift: the county prosecutor chose not to press charges against Margarite herself, but three students involved in the case, including Isaiah and two of the girls who forwarded Margarite's photo, were charged with distributing child pornography—a Class C felony. All these students were in eighth grade.[22]

Attempts to curb the crisis of sexting and "self-pornification" have generally taken three forms: "prosecutorial, pedagogical, and technological."[23] Cases like the one involving Margarite have set out to prosecute sexting as a criminal offense. Educators are attempting to create awareness of the dangers of sexting. And tech companies are writing software that allows parents to monitor the cyber-life of their children.[24] But some argue these strategies rely too heavily on worst-case scenarios and will, in the end, be as effective (or ineffective) as similar campaigns against drug use. "A more sophisticated approach requires an examination of the forces that compel teenagers to share these images in the first place."[25]

What motivates young people to participate in sexting when the consequences can be so severe? Obvious answers include a desire to flirt or gain popularity, to meet the requests or demands of a significant other, and to explore and express sexuality in a playful but not-yet-actualized sexual activity. But this is an incomplete picture. Teen sexting takes place within a larger system where teens replicate broader social behavior.[26]

Self-pornification is a result of teens and young adults coming of age in an increasingly pornified American culture that "encourages and rewards the pornographic impulse. Take the examples of self-pornographers like Kim Kardashian, Pamela Anderson and Paris Hilton, all of whom have been generously rewarded for their public displays of private moments."[27]

When adolescents are taught, largely through the mass media, that sexual experience is a desired good, and these values are then perpetuated among their peers, it seems clear that portraying oneself as sexual would be a desirable strategy.[28]

In American popular media and advertising, women's bodies are routinely sexualized and objectified. These images promote the message that a woman's identity and worth depend heavily on how physically attractive and sexy she appears.[29] It's not hard to imagine that these cultural messages contribute to the sexting phenomenon. But these aren't the only messages young people receive. "Their superiors—teachers, parents, legislators, and law enforcement agents—expect from them a degree of moral purity and ethical exactitude that is demanded from no other social group."[30]

The message of purity culture is, ironically, not so different from our overly sexualized popular media culture: for both, a woman's worth lies in her ability, or her refusal, to be overtly sexual. Both approaches teach American girls that their bodies and their sexuality are what make them valuable.[31]

The sexting crisis embodies the contradictions and complications teens face in a world that is pulling them in opposite directions. And dealing with the epidemic of sexting must take into account these complexities. Approaches must send a strong message of deterrence that includes not only the dangers and consequences of sexting, but casts a vision for identity and sexuality that challenges pornified popular culture.

WHO LOOKS AND HOW OFTEN?

1 OUT OF 3 AMERICANS SEEK OUT PORN AT LEAST ONCE A MONTH

6%	14%	13%	18%	49%
Daily	Weekly	Once or twice a month	Less often	Never

AGE, GENDER AND FAITH PRACTICE ARE THE THREE BIGGEST FACTORS IN FREQUENT PORN USE

% combined of those who report seeking out porn daily, weekly and monthly

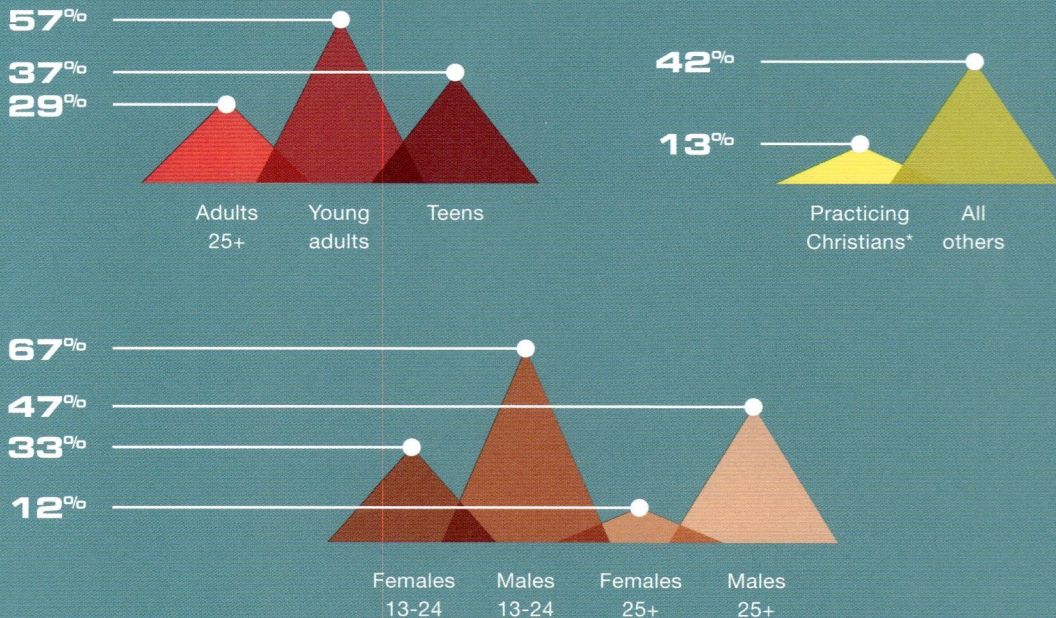

- 57%
- 37%
- 29%

Adults 25+ — Young adults — Teens

- 42%
- 13%

Practicing Christians* — All others

- 67%
- 47%
- 33%
- 12%

Females 13-24 — Males 13-24 — Females 25+ — Males 25+

*It is likely practicing Christians use porn less frequently, as reported, but there may also be under-reporting since porn use within the Christian community is much less socially acceptable than in the wider culture.

IN OTHER WORDS, IF YOU'RE A YOUNG MAN WHO IS NOT A PRACTICING CHRISTIAN, YOU PROBABLY USE PORN REGULARLY

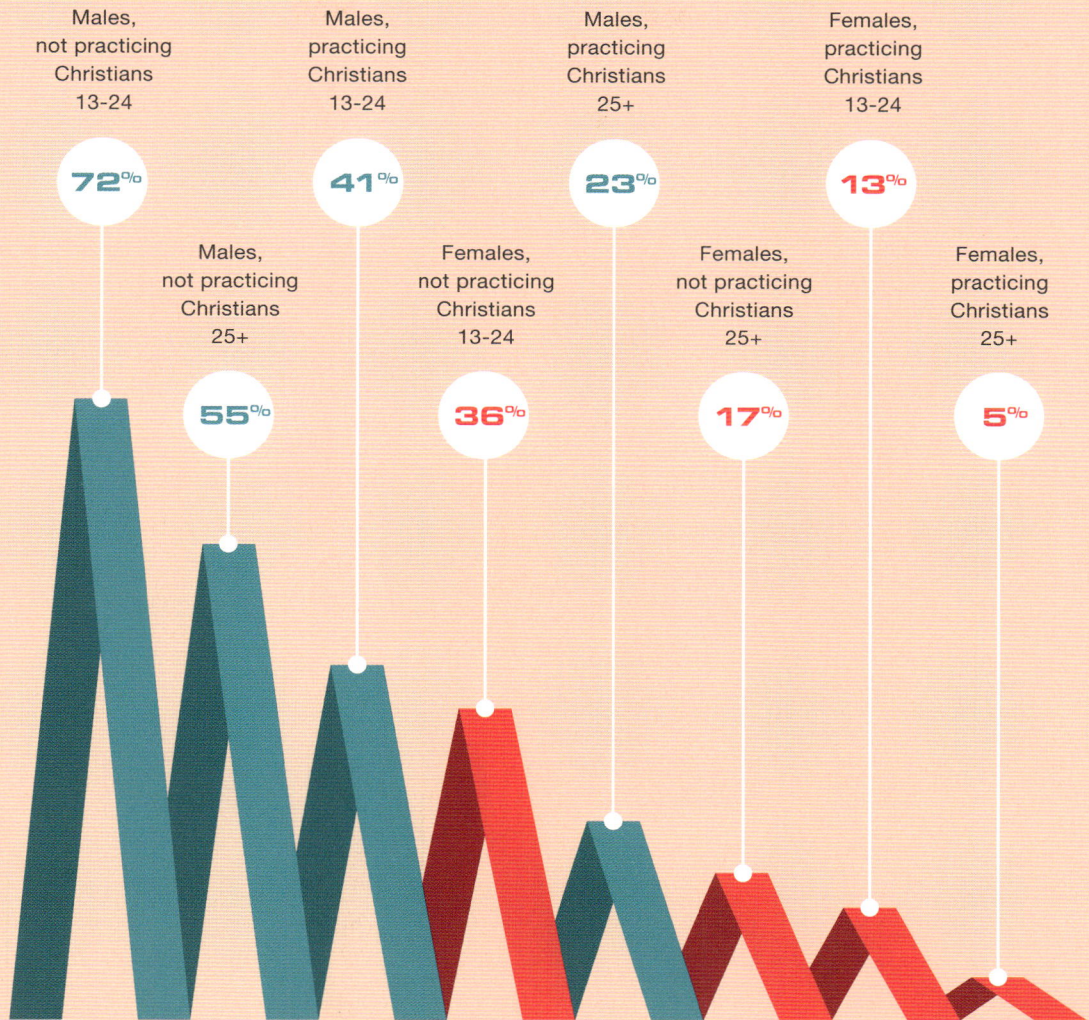

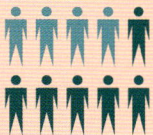

Males, not practicing Christians 13-24 — **72%**

Males, practicing Christians 13-24 — **41%**

Males, practicing Christians 25+ — **23%**

Females, practicing Christians 13-24 — **13%**

Males, not practicing Christians 25+ — **55%**

Females, not practicing Christians 13-24 — **36%**

Females, not practicing Christians 25+ — **17%**

Females, practicing Christians 25+ — **5%**

However, it's important for Christian leaders—especially youth and young adult pastors—to notice that the people who are third most likely to use porn are teen/young adult males in the Church. While they are still well below their peers who are not practicing Christians in frequency of porn use, four in 10 of them are actively seeking it out at least once or twice a month.

DIFFERENT PEOPLE USE PORN FOR DIFFERENT REASONS

Not surprisingly, "personal arousal" is the #1 reason people use porn. But after that, things get interesting.

- 🔵 Personal arousal
- 🔴 Boredom
- 🟡 Curiosity
- 🟤 It's just fun
- ⚪ To get tips or ideas
- 🔵 Set the mood with my significant other
- 🔴 Less risky than having sex
- 🟢 To express my sexuality

BY GENERATION

Teens

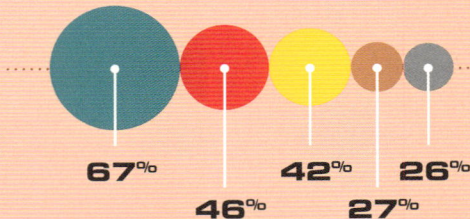

67% 46% 42% 27% 26%

Young adults

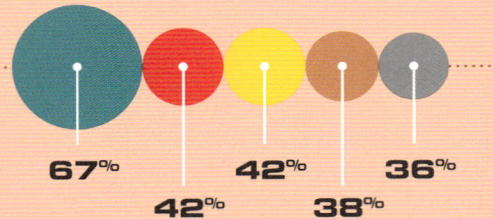

67% 42% 42% 38% 36%

older Millennials

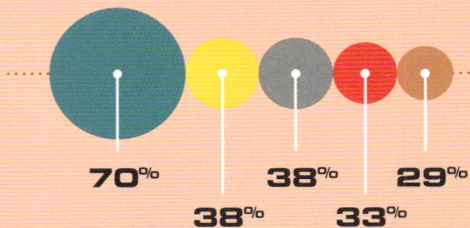

70% 38% 38% 33% 29%

Gen-Xers

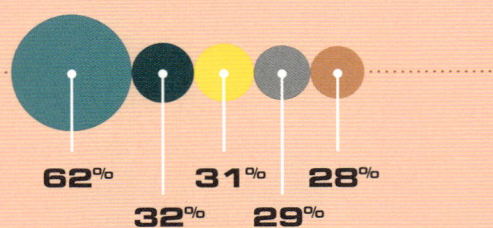

62% 32% 31% 29% 28%

Boomers

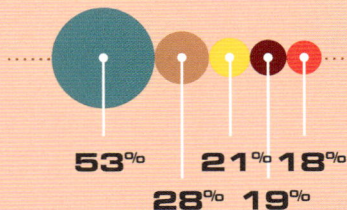

53% 28% 21% 19% 18%

BY LIFESTAGE

Married

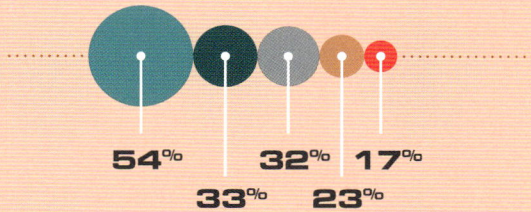

54% 33% 32% 23% 17%

Single, never married

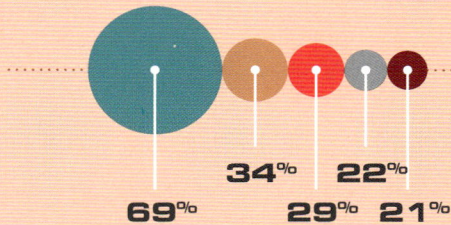

69% 34% 29% 22% 21%

Single, no longer married

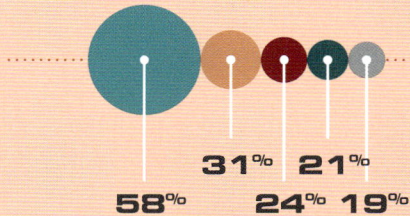

58% 31% 24% 21% 19%

BY ETHNICITY

Asian

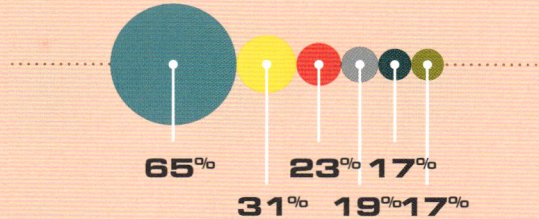

65% 31% 23% 19% 17% 17%

Hispanic

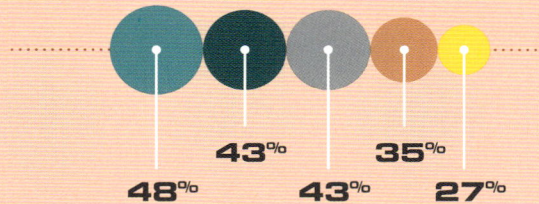

48% 43% 43% 35% 27%

Black

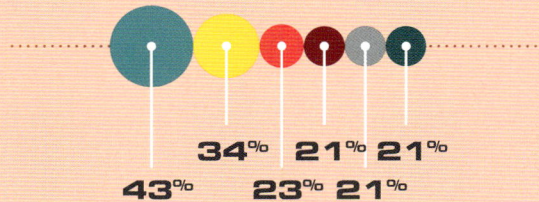

43% 34% 23% 21% 21% 21%

White

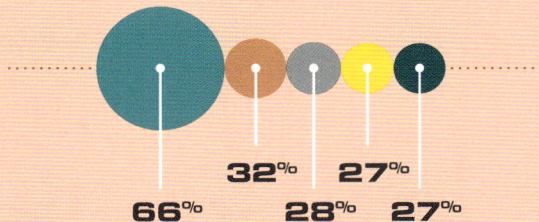

66% 32% 28% 27% 27%

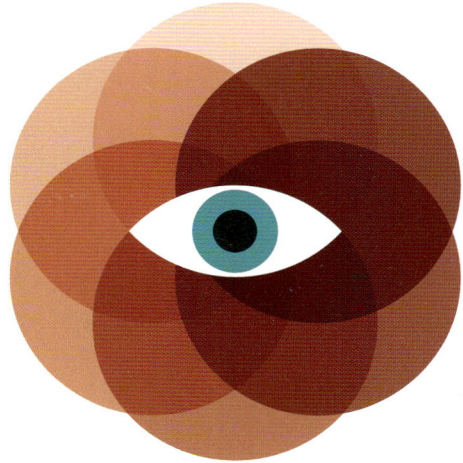

2.

THE USES OF PORN

How often do people view porn?

This is not an easy question to answer. Living in a hyper-sexualized and pornified media culture means that catching sight of explicit images requires little effort. People often come across images they never intended to see through online newsfeeds, pop-up advertisements, emails, texts, search engines, billboards and signs, and many more inputs. A constant stream of images vying for your attention means that "viewing" requires extra thought—an intent—to actually focus on and *see* the image. Without this kind of focused attention, sexually charged images are like driving by a forest: You know you're passing trees but, if you don't stop and take a look, your brain only registers a blur of green.

Consequently, rather than asking how often people "view" porn—a general and vague measure of porn use—Barna created a way to triangulate data related to seeing porn and a person's *intention* to view porn. As previously discussed, the intent

LIVING IN A
HYPERSEXUALIZED
AND PORNIFIED MEDIA
CULTURE MEANS THAT
CATCHING SIGHT
OF EXPLICIT
IMAGES REQUIRES
LITTLE EFFORT

behind viewing an image is critical for determining whether an image is considered porn. Applying this reasoning to frequency of views, researchers parsed the data based on a person's intent.

To measure frequency of porn use in the United States, Barna asked a nationally representative panel ages 13 and older 1) how often they "come across" porn, even if they are not seeking it out, and 2) how often they "actively seek out" porn. The first question ignores any intent to view porn and so returns the highest possible percentage of frequency. The latter question focuses only on intentional viewing and thus returns the lower percentage.

51%
of all Americans
seek out porn at
least occasionally

FREQUENCY OF PORN VIEWING
% among U.S. teens, young adults and adults 25+

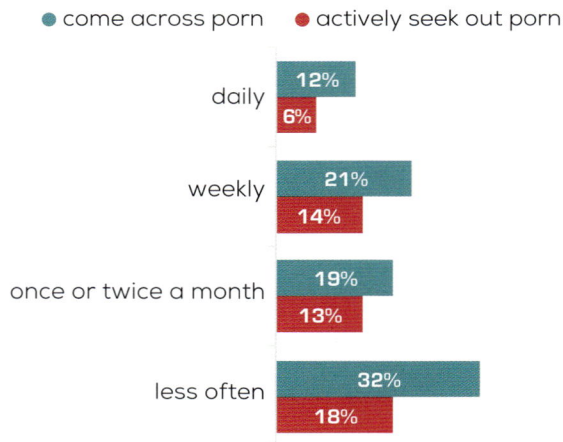

● come across porn   ● actively seek out porn

	come across porn	actively seek out porn
daily	12%	6%
weekly	21%	14%
once or twice a month	19%	13%
less often	32%	18%

Between 6 and 12 percent of people ages 13 and older view porn daily; 14 to 21 percent view porn weekly; 13 to 19 percent view it once or twice a month; and 18 to 32 percent view it less often. Half of the cohort (49%) says they never seek out porn, and 17 percent say they have never come across it.

COMING ACROSS VS. SEEKING OUT

Smartphones, tablets and laptops have revolutionized the way we encounter images; pictures and videos are easily accessible with one swipe or click. The ubiquity of online pornography, coupled with open and unlimited access to information and imagery through new media and technology, are key reasons people stumble onto pornography on a regular basis. It doesn't take much effort to encounter sexually explicit content on apps like Snapchat and Instagram, or even via text messaging (some of which is unsolicited).

Pornified images in mainstream media, including in video games, increase a person's chances of encountering sexually explicit material. Popular culture is awash in sexualized images and ideas; you only need to see an Axe commercial, Miley Cyrus performance or "reality" show like *The Bachelor* for confirmation.[32]

The "pornification" of pop culture is, at least in some ways, the byproduct of a broader cultural shift against authority and objectivity, particularly in youth culture, that manifests in self-expression, subjectivity and experimentation.[33] The normalization of porn is creating a hypersexualized culture in which younger generations are now coming of age. They, in turn, tend to be more open to sexual experimentation and self-expression—leading to further social acceptance of sexually explicit content. It's unclear where (or if) this self-perpetuating feedback loop will end.

The more frequently a person consumes pornography online or through Internet-connected apps, the more he or she is targeted through ad networks that use cookies—little packets of data on his or her device that track online activity and browsing history and then share that information with advertisers and retailers. The more porn a person consumes, the more invitations he or she receives to consume porn.

It's sobering that the more you seek porn, the more porn seeks you. Pornographers load up a person's computer up with cookies that alert other porn distributors to your interest. It's a system designed to transform the casual user into an addict. Could we use the same approach? What would it look like to think about escaping porn addiction in a similar "systemic" way?

YOUNGER GENERATIONS TEND TO BE MORE OPEN TO SEXUAL EXPERIMENTATION AND SELF-EXPRESSION

The data clearly shows that the more frequently a person actively seeks porn, the more frequently he or she will come across porn—even when he or she is not actively searching for it. Researchers cross-referenced how frequently someone comes across porn with how often someone seeks it out—*and found a direct correlation.* If a person seeks out porn on a daily basis, he or she is more likely to come across porn on a daily basis. The same goes for those who seek out porn weekly, once or twice a month and less often. The darker squares in the table below show that those who seek porn daily are more likely than others to come across it daily (73%); those who seek porn weekly are more likely than others to come across it weekly (54%); and so on.

CORRELATIONS BETWEEN *SEEKING OUT* AND *COMING ACROSS* PORN

% among U.S. teens, young adults and adults 25+

How often do you come across porn?		% never	% less often	% once or twice a month	% weekly	% daily
	daily	5%	11%	15%	16%	73%
	weekly	12%	20%	22%	54%	14%
	once or twice a month	13%	25%	36%	14%	3%
	less often	41%	42%	17%	13%	8%
	never	28%	2%	10%	2%	2%

How often do you actively seek out porn?

Coming across porn frequently does *not* necessarily correlate to frequently seeking it out. That is, just because a person comes across porn doesn't mean he or she is more prone to seek it out.

Age, gender, income level, ethnicity, marital status and faith practice all seem to affect how often people use porn. In the following sections, we examine each of these demographic variables.

Porn Use by Age

When it comes to coming across porn, as opposed to actively seeking it out, the differences between teens (ages 13 to 17), older Millennials (25 to 30) and Gen-Xers (31 to 50) are statistically insignificant. However, the percentage among young adults 18 to 24 is significantly higher than other age segments. Since actively searching for porn increases one's chances of coming across porn—and young adults are more likely than others to seek it out—this result is as expected.

57%
of young adults
seek porn at least
once a month

HOW FREQUENTLY PEOPLE COME ACROSS VS. SEEK OUT PORN, BY AGE

% among U.S. teens, young adults and adults 25+

● daily ● weekly ● once or twice a month ● less often ● never

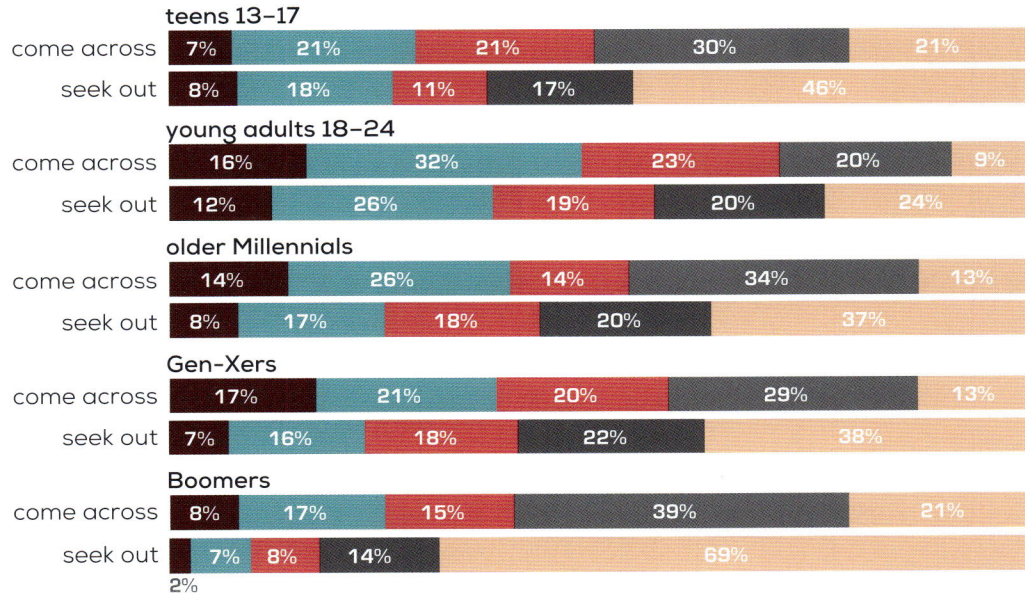

teens 13–17

	daily	weekly	once or twice a month	less often	never
come across	7%	21%	21%	30%	21%
seek out	8%	18%	11%	17%	46%

young adults 18–24

	daily	weekly	once or twice a month	less often	never
come across	16%	32%	23%	20%	9%
seek out	12%	26%	19%	20%	24%

older Millennials

	daily	weekly	once or twice a month	less often	never
come across	14%	26%	14%	34%	13%
seek out	8%	17%	18%	20%	37%

Gen-Xers

	daily	weekly	once or twice a month	less often	never
come across	17%	21%	20%	29%	13%
seek out	7%	16%	18%	22%	38%

Boomers

	daily	weekly	once or twice a month	less often	never
come across	8%	17%	15%	39%	21%
seek out	2%	7%	8%	14%	69%

Young adults may also come across porn more frequently than other age cohorts because they tend to have more "comprehensive" notions of what qualifies as porn. This may seem counterintuitive, but in four out of five scenarios young adults are more likely than older adults to classify an image as porn. Consequently, when people of different ages see the same image, the younger person is a bit more likely to perceive the image in question as porn.

WHAT IS *DEFINITELY* PORN?, BY GENERATION

% "definitely" among U.S. adults 18 and older

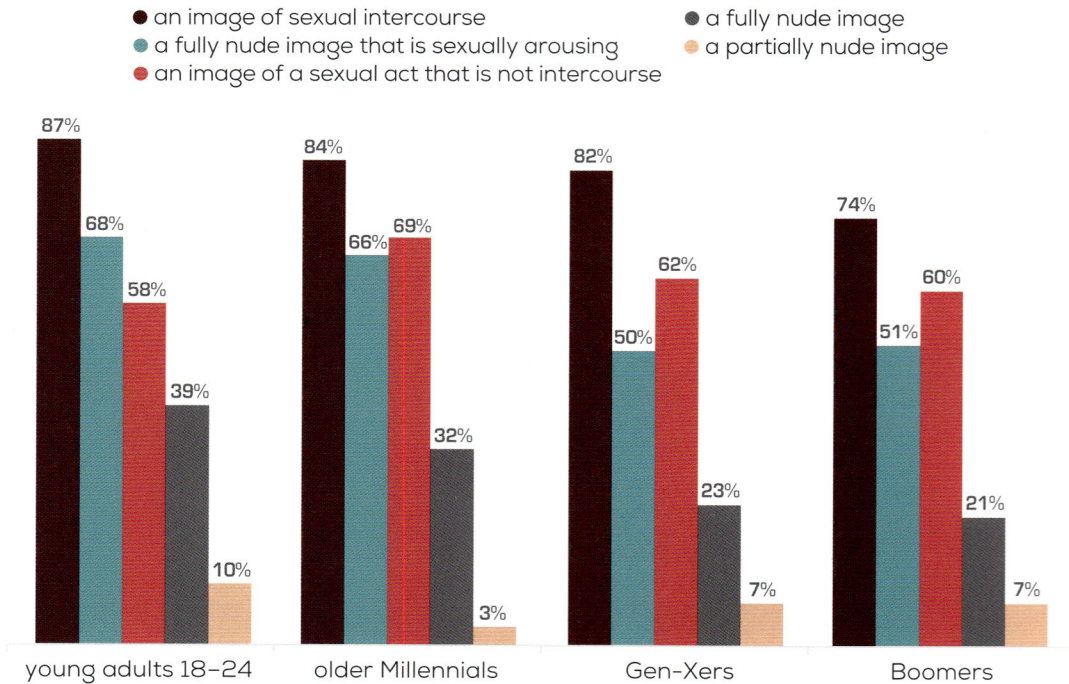

- ● an image of sexual intercourse
- ● a fully nude image
- ● a fully nude image that is sexually arousing
- ● a partially nude image
- ● an image of a sexual act that is not intercourse

	young adults 18–24	older Millennials	Gen-Xers	Boomers
an image of sexual intercourse	87%	84%	82%	74%
a fully nude image that is sexually arousing	68%	66%	50%	51%
an image of a sexual act that is not intercourse	58%	69%	62%	60%
a fully nude image	39%	32%	23%	21%
a partially nude image	10%	3%	7%	7%

Teens are less active than young adults in seeking out porn and somewhat on par with older Millennials and Gen-Xers. Every age cohort under the age of 50 is more likely than Boomers (51 to 69) to seek out porn.

It is likely that limited access to technology, thanks to vigilant parents, plays some role in teens' less frequent searches compared to young adults. After all, it is more difficult to find porn if you don't have your own personal laptop, smartphone or tablet! It is even more difficult if parents filter and block Internet access and monitor their teen's online footprint. (And there are only so many days in a week when a kid can watch porn at a friend's house without their parents finding out.)

LIMITED ACCESS TO TECHNOLOGY, THANKS TO VIGILANT PARENTS, LIKELY PLAYS SOME ROLE IN TEENS' LESS FREQUENT SEARCHES FOR PORN

PORN USE BY GENDER

Men come across porn more frequently than women, even when they are not actively seeking it out. In fact, they are five times more likely to come across porn on a daily basis (20% of men vs. 4% of women). Women (25%), on the other hand, are more than twice as likely as men (10%) to say they never come across porn. Why are men so much more likely to come across porn than women? The simplest explanation is they are more likely, by a wide margin, to actively search for porn. Two-thirds of men 25 and older say they seek porn at least occasionally (66%), compared to only 27 percent of women.

46%
of men seek out porn at least once a month

HOW FREQUENTLY PEOPLE COME ACROSS VS. SEEK OUT PORN, BY GENDER
% among U.S. adults 25+

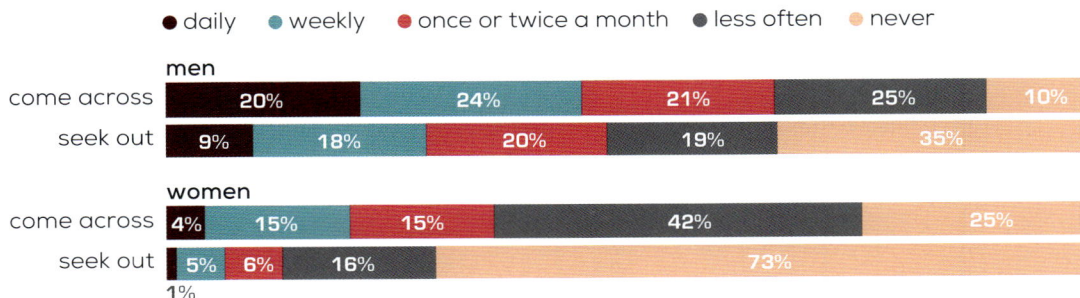

● daily   ● weekly   ● once or twice a month   ● less often   ● never

men

come across	20%	24%	21%	25%	10%
seek out	9%	18%	20%	19%	35%

women

come across	4%	15%	15%	42%	25%
seek out	5%	6%	16%		73%

1%

PORN USE BY MARITAL STATUS

On the whole, it is probably accurate to say married people have easier access than single people to sex. Married couples do not necessarily engage in more sexual activity than singles, but overall they have fewer barriers to connecting with a sexual partner. Consequently, it is not altogether surprising that singles are more prone to porn use than those who are married.

Six in 10 married adults say they never actively seek out porn (60%), but the same is true of only 44 percent of singles. Singles seek out porn on a daily basis twice as often as married adults. This may indicate an attempt to substitute sexual intimacy with porn, especially for singles who are not in a serious relationship.

HOW FREQUENTLY PEOPLE COME ACROSS VS. SEEK OUT PORN, BY MARITAL STATUS
% among U.S. adults 25+

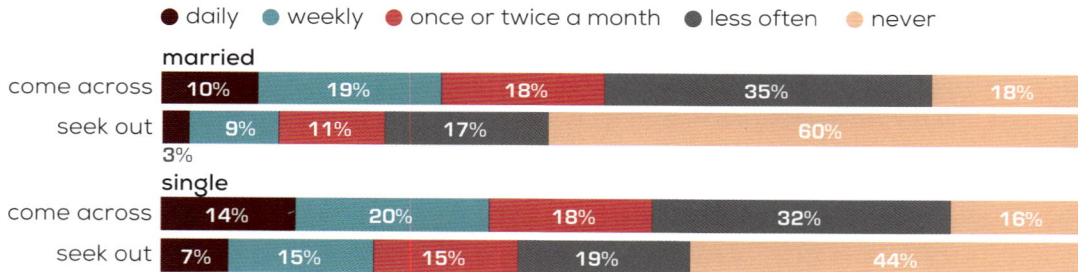

● daily ● weekly ● once or twice a month ● less often ● never

married

	daily	weekly	once or twice a month	less often	never
come across	10%	19%	18%	35%	18%
seek out	3%	9%	11%	17%	60%

single

	daily	weekly	once or twice a month	less often	never
come across	14%	20%	18%	32%	16%
seek out	7%	15%	15%	19%	44%

PORN USE BY INCOME LEVEL

When it comes to coming across and seeking out porn, a middle income between $50,000 and $99,000 per year tends to correlate with more views. The reasons for this are unclear, but may relate to greater access to technology than lower income Americans and less access to more expensive activities than higher income Americans.

HOW FREQUENTLY PEOPLE COME ACROSS VS. SEEK OUT PORN, BY INCOME LEVEL

% among U.S. adults 25+

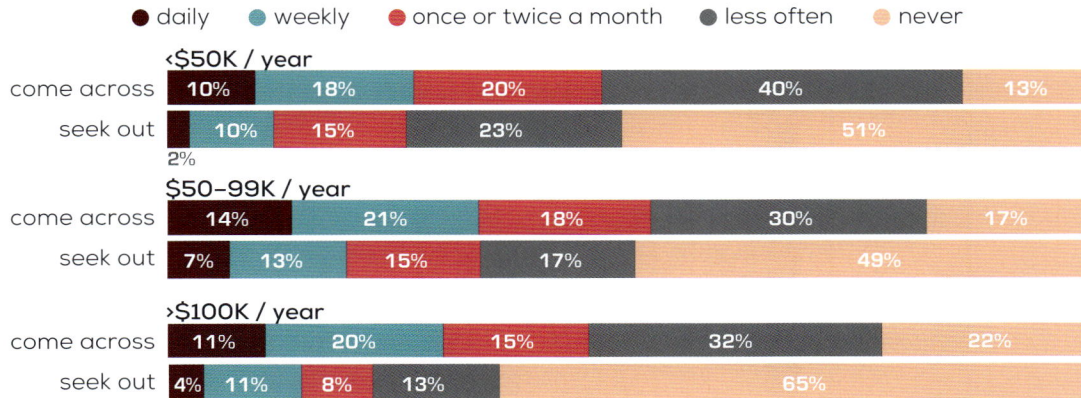

● daily   ● weekly   ● once or twice a month   ● less often   ● never

<$50K / year

	daily	weekly	once or twice a month	less often	never
come across	10%	18%	20%	40%	13%
seek out	10%	15%	23%	51%	2%

$50–99K / year

	daily	weekly	once or twice a month	less often	never
come across	14%	21%	18%	30%	17%
seek out	7%	13%	15%	17%	49%

>$100K / year

	daily	weekly	once or twice a month	less often	never
come across	11%	20%	15%	32%	22%
seek out	4%	11%	8%	13%	65%

PORN USE BY ETHNICITY*

Black and Hispanic adults seem to come across porn at an alarmingly high rate compared with white and Asian adults. While Hispanics are also more likely than other ethnic cohorts to search for porn daily—which likely leads to more unintended encounters with porn, as previously discussed—it is unclear why black Americans come across porn so frequently. While whites (8% vs. 4%), Hispanics (22% vs. 11%) and Asians (11% vs. 4%) say they come across porn roughly twice as often as they seek it out, black adults report coming across porn *13 times more frequently* than they seek it out (26% vs. 2%). This is an enormous disparity, and the reasons for it are unclear.

In 1 Corinthians 6:15 Paul says that a member of the body of Christ who sexually unites with a prostitute unites Christ to the sexual act. Is porn use the same thing in a more contemporary form? If so, what does that mean for the Church?

*Sample sizes of black, Hispanic and Asian cohorts of adults 25 and older were small enough that Barna would not usually include this data for analysis. However, because the data seem to indicate significant divergences between ethnic groups, we have chosen to release these results with a caveat noting the small sample sizes.

HOW FREQUENTLY PEOPLE COME ACROSS VS. SEEK OUT PORN, BY ETHNICITY

% among U.S. adults 25+

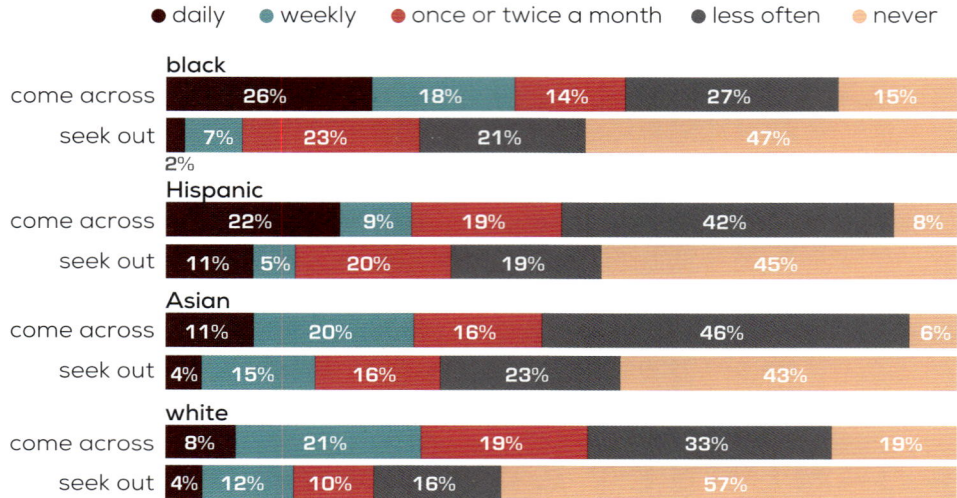

● daily ● weekly ● once or twice a month ● less often ● never

black

	daily	weekly	once or twice a month	less often	never
come across	26%	18%	14%	27%	15%
seek out	2%	7%	23%	21%	47%

Hispanic

	daily	weekly	once or twice a month	less often	never
come across	22%	9%	19%	42%	8%
seek out	11%	5%	20%	19%	45%

Asian

	daily	weekly	once or twice a month	less often	never
come across	11%	20%	16%	46%	6%
seek out	4%	15%	16%	23%	43%

white

	daily	weekly	once or twice a month	less often	never
come across	8%	21%	19%	33%	19%
seek out	4%	12%	10%	16%	57%

PORN USE BY FAITH PRACTICE

Under Barna's definition, *practicing Christians* are self-identified Christians who agree strongly that their faith is very important in their life and have attended a church worship service within the past month. (Self-identified Christians who do not meet these criteria are called *non-practicing Christians*.) Practicing Christians report coming across porn somewhat *less* frequently than other Americans. Just 9 percent of practicing Christians, for example, come across porn on a daily basis compared to 14 percent among the rest of the population. Likewise, 17 percent of practicing Christians say they come across porn weekly, compared to 23 percent among those who are not practicing Christians.

Besides the obvious explanation—that practicing Christians seek porn less often than others, and so come across it less often—

porn-blocking filters, which make it less likely for a device user to unintentionally stumble across porn, are also more common among practicing Christians. Seventeen percent who have sought out porn in the past report installing such filters on all their devices, compared to only 11 percent among all adults who have ever searched for porn.

Practicing Christians do, indeed, seek out porn much less frequently than other teens and adults. Just 2 percent search for porn daily, compared to 8 percent of other Americans; 5 percent search weekly, compared to 17 percent among the rest of the population; and 6 percent seek out porn once or twice a month, compared to 17 percent of all others. Seven in 10 practicing Christians (72%) report never searching for porn, compared to 39 percent of those who do not practice Christianity.

PRACTICING CHRISTIANS SEEK OUT PORN MUCH LESS FREQUENTLY THAN OTHER TEENS AND ADULTS

13% of practicing Christians seek porn at least once a month, compared to 42% of all others

HOW FREQUENTLY PEOPLE COME ACROSS VS. SEEK OUT PORN, BY FAITH PRACTICE

% among U.S. teens, young adults and adults 25+

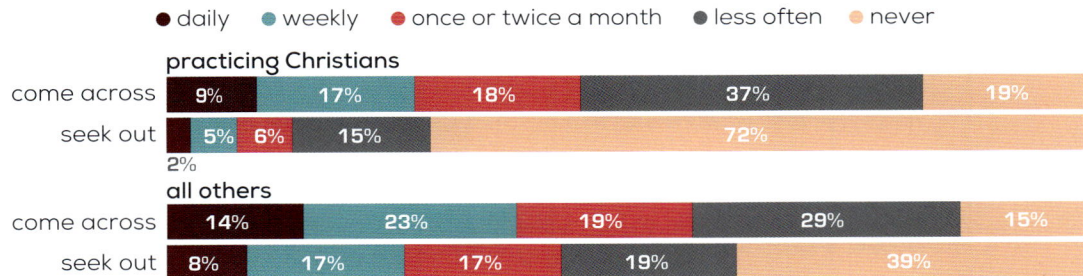

● daily ● weekly ● once or twice a month ● less often ● never

practicing Christians

	daily	weekly	once or twice a month	less often	never
come across	9%	17%	18%	37%	19%
seek out	2%	5%	6%	15%	72%

all others

	daily	weekly	once or twice a month	less often	never
come across	14%	23%	19%	29%	15%
seek out	8%	17%	17%	19%	39%

Barna researchers wondered which factor of practicing faith (if any) has a greater impact on how frequently one seeks out porn: 1) church attendance or 2) having a faith that is important to one's life. It turns out that infrequent church attendance is not a significant factor when it comes to porn use. A low-priority faith, however, *is* strongly correlated with more frequent porn seeking. In fact, self-identified Christians who do not consider their faith important are *more likely than the national average* to seek out porn daily, weekly and once or twice a month.

HOW FREQUENTLY PEOPLE SEEK OUT PORN, BY CHURCH ATTENDANCE & FAITH PRIORITY

% among U.S. teens, young adults and adults 25+

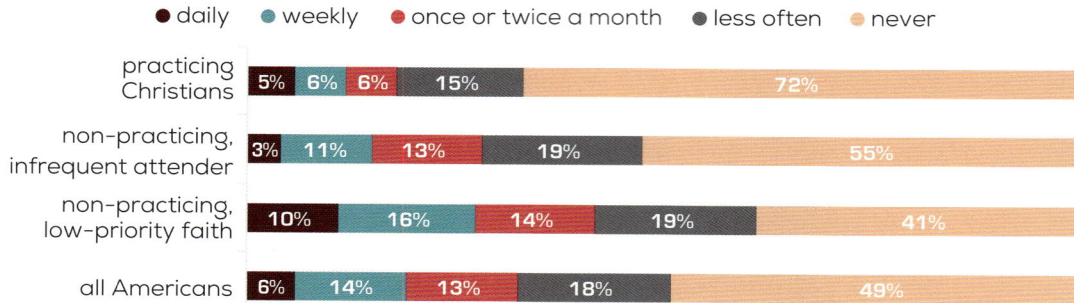

● daily ● weekly ● once or twice a month ● less often ● never

	daily	weekly	once or twice a month	less often	never
practicing Christians	5%	6%	6%	15%	72%
non-practicing, infrequent attender	3%	11%	13%	19%	55%
non-practicing, low-priority faith	10%	16%	14%	19%	41%
all Americans	6%	14%	13%	18%	49%

WHY PEOPLE USE PORN

WITHOUT RECOGNIZING THE REASONS THAT COMPEL PEOPLE TO USE PORNOGRAPHY, IT'S IMPOSSIBLE TO KNOW WHAT SPIRITUAL, RELATIONAL OR EMOTIONAL NEEDS LIE AT THE ROOT OF THEIR COMPULSION

How often do people view porn? is an important question. Even more important, however, is *why* they view it. As discussed in the previous chapter, function takes precedence over form. Without recognizing the reasons that compel people to use pornography—regardless of how often they use it—it's impossible to know what spiritual, relational or emotional needs lie at the root of their compulsion.

With this in mind, let's examine the reasons people say they use porn, and look at some of the differences between groups.

The most common reason among both teens and adults is *personal arousal* (63%). Other top reasons include "curiosity" (33%), "it's just fun" (30%), "to get tips or ideas for my own sex life" (29%), "boredom" (27%) and "to set the mood with a spouse / girlfriend / boyfriend / partner" (24%). (There are significant generational differences that we'll explore, as well.)

REASONS PEOPLE SEARCH FOR PORN

base: U.S. teens and adults 13 and older who have ever actively sought out porn (multiple response)	% total
for personal arousal	63
curiosity	33
it's just fun	30
to get tips or ideas for my own sex life	29
boredom	27
to set the mood with a spouse / girlfriend / boyfriend / partner	24
it's less risky than actually having sex	15
to express my sexuality	14
no particular reason	5
haven't thought about it	3
because my friend(s) do(es)	1

Among those who view porn for personal arousal, 13 percent actively seek it out on a daily basis, 29 percent do so weekly, 33 percent once or twice a month and 26 percent less often. The majority searches for porn weekly or monthly (62%).

There is a high correlation between frequent use and doing so for personal arousal. Among those who seek out porn on a daily basis, 80 percent do so for personal arousal. Among those who search weekly, 75 percent do so for personal arousal. And among those who seek it out once or twice a month, 69 percent do so for personal arousal.

Jesus taught that looking at a woman lustfully is equal to committing adultery, and he hyperbolically counseled plucking out your eye to avoid it. In a broad sense, Jesus was warning against seeing others through a haze of self-centered desire rather than with eyes of godly love. Are there ways in which the Church participates in the culture of objectification, treating people as "useful for me" instead of "valuable to God"? Against the swift current of a culture obsessed with self-fulfillment, how can we teach others and ourselves to love according to the 1 Corinthians 13 model?

Those who search for porn because "it's just fun" are more likely to view porn on a daily basis (56%). Somewhat similarly, "to express my sexuality" is most common among those who use porn daily (27%) or weekly (23%), but less so among those who do so once or twice a month (10%) or less often (7%).

REASONS PEOPLE SEARCH FOR PORN, BY FREQUENCY OF USE

	% daily	% weekly	% once or twice a month	% less often
base: U.S. teen and adults 13 and older who have ever actively sought out porn (multiple response)				
for personal arousal	80	75	69	43
it's just fun	56	38	30	16
to get tips or ideas for my own sex life	31	32	32	23
boredom	27	34	32	19
curiosity	27	26	36	37
to express my sexuality	27	23	10	7
it's less risky than actually having sex	26	17	16	10
to set the mood with a spouse / girlfriend / boyfriend / partner	22	22	30	20

Reasons by Age

Personal arousal is the top reason—*function*—among all age cohorts for using porn. But there are clear generational differences when it comes to other motivations. (See the following page.) Teens and young adults, for example, are most likely to use porn as a remedy for boredom. Gen-Xers, on the other hand, are most likely among the generations to have children under 18 living at home—which may account for "boredom" being low on their list of motivations for porn use! Gen-Xers stand out as most likely to use porn to set the mood with a significant other. (In fact, all adults with children under 18 living at home—whether married or single—are more likely than those with no children at home to use porn to set the mood with a significant other.)

Reasons by Gender

Conforming somewhat to relational typecasting, a higher percentage of women (41%) than men (21%) say they view porn to set the mood with a significant other or to get tips or ideas for their own sex life (34% vs. 23% of men). They're also more likely to say they view porn out of curiosity (36%). A lower percentage of women (55%) than men (63%) say they view porn for personal arousal and because "it's just fun" (17% vs. 33%).

REASONS PEOPLE SEARCH FOR PORN, BY GENDER

	% men	% women
base: adults 25+ who have ever actively sought out porn *(multiple response)*		
for personal arousal	63	55
it's just fun	33	17
curiosity	26	36
to get tips or ideas for my own sex life	23	34
to set the mood with a significant other	21	41

REASONS PEOPLE SEARCH FOR PORN, BY AGE

% among U.S. teens and adults 13 and older who actively seek out porn

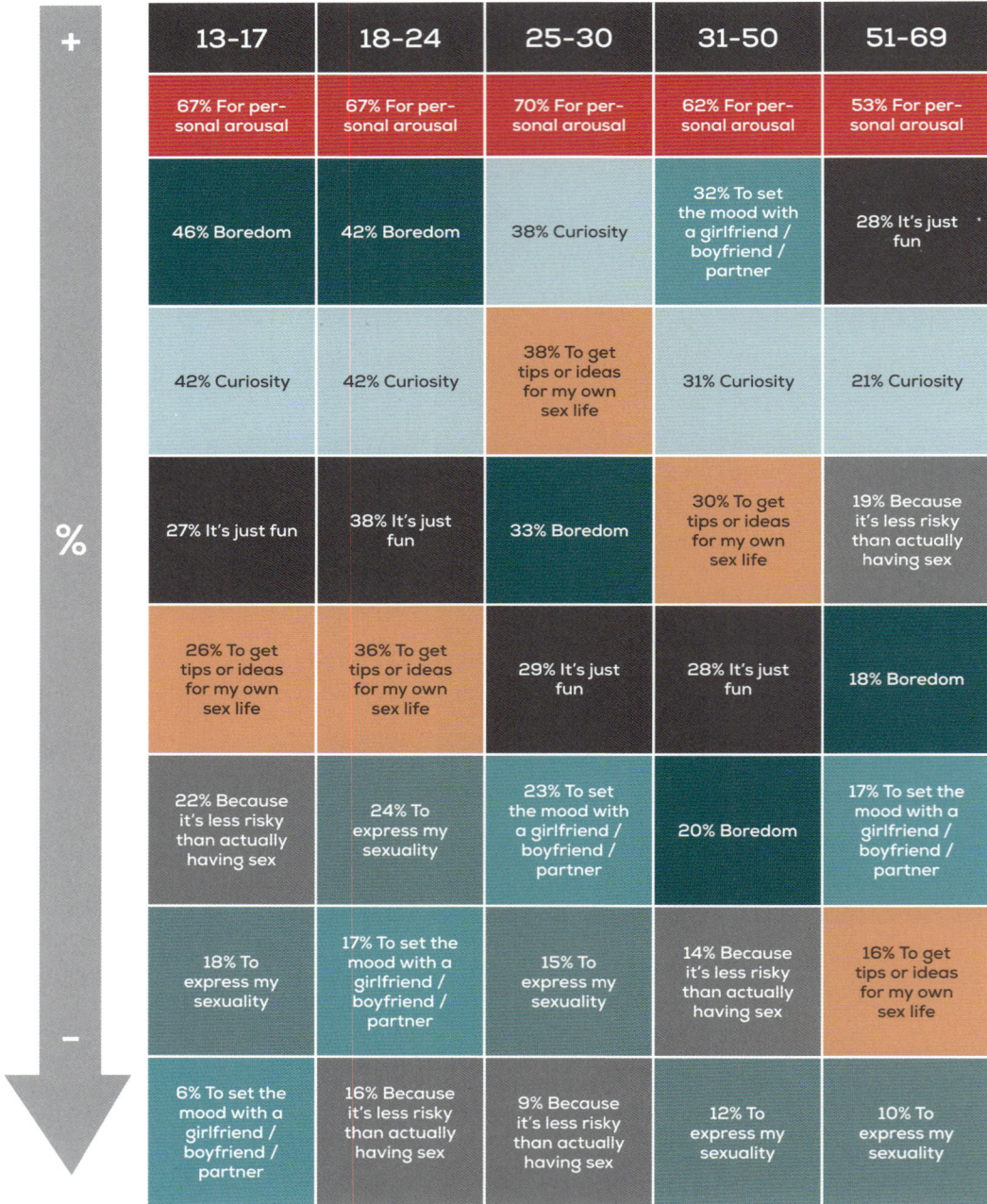

	13-17	18-24	25-30	31-50	51-69
+	67% For personal arousal	67% For personal arousal	70% For personal arousal	62% For personal arousal	53% For personal arousal
	46% Boredom	42% Boredom	38% Curiosity	32% To set the mood with a girlfriend / boyfriend / partner	28% It's just fun
	42% Curiosity	42% Curiosity	38% To get tips or ideas for my own sex life	31% Curiosity	21% Curiosity
%	27% It's just fun	38% It's just fun	33% Boredom	30% To get tips or ideas for my own sex life	19% Because it's less risky than actually having sex
	26% To get tips or ideas for my own sex life	36% To get tips or ideas for my own sex life	29% It's just fun	28% It's just fun	18% Boredom
	22% Because it's less risky than actually having sex	24% To express my sexuality	23% To set the mood with a girlfriend / boyfriend / partner	20% Boredom	17% To set the mood with a girlfriend / boyfriend / partner
	18% To express my sexuality	17% To set the mood with a girlfriend / boyfriend / partner	15% To express my sexuality	14% Because it's less risky than actually having sex	16% To get tips or ideas for my own sex life
−	6% To set the mood with a girlfriend / boyfriend / partner	16% Because it's less risky than actually having sex	9% Because it's less risky than actually having sex	12% To express my sexuality	10% To express my sexuality

Reasons by Marital Status

Those who have never been married (69%) are more likely than those who are currently married (54%) or who have been married in the past (58%) but are currently divorced, widowed or separated to cite personal arousal as their main reason for using porn. Using porn out of boredom is also more common among never marrieds (29%) than among those who are now married (17%) or have been at some point in the past (14%).

REASONS PEOPLE SEARCH FOR PORN, BY MARITAL STATUS

base: adults 25+ who have ever actively sought out porn (multiple response)	% married	% all single	% never married	% single, have been married
for personal arousal	54	66	69	57
to set the mood with a spouse / girlfriend / boyfriend / partner	33	21	20	20
to get tips or ideas for my own sex life	32	21	22	17
curiosity	28	29	29	30
it's just fun	23	33	34	32
boredom	17	25	29	14
to express my sexuality	12	10	10	12
it's less risky than actually having sex	6	22	21	22

Reasons by Ethnicity

Black and Hispanic adults are less likely than whites and Asians to use porn for personal arousal. Compared to other ethnic cohorts, Hispanic adults report using porn more frequently to set the mood with their partner (43%) or to get tips or ideas for their own sex life (43%). This "sex aid" approach to porn may explain why Hispanics are more likely to seek it out on a daily basis.

REASONS PEOPLE SEARCH FOR PORN, BY ETHNICITY

	% black	% Hispanic	% Asian	% white
base: adults 25+ who have ever actively sought out porn (multiple response)				
for personal arousal	43	48	65	66
it's just fun	12	35	14	32
to get tips or ideas for my own sex life	21	43	19	28
curiosity	34	27	31	27
to set the mood with a spouse/ girlfriend / boyfriend / partner	21	43	17	27
boredom	23	19	23	22
it's less risky than actually having sex	21	15	6	15
to express my sexuality	4	13	17	13
no particular reason	14	1	9	5

MINISTERING TO THE WHYS

Consider how you and your faith community address porn use. How well do you focus on the *reasons* different people use it and tailor your ministry approach accordingly? For example, since teens and young adults often cite "boredom" as their reason for seeking porn, is it possible there is a spiritual gap in their lives? Perhaps they do not know how to be quiet, able to rest and enjoy God's presence in stillness. Training Christians in the spiritual disciplines of prayer and silence is something the Church has done for centuries—can your church do the same for the young people in your community, so they can be free of the restlessness that prompts them to fill every second with distraction?

Or consider the single adults in your church who may use porn as "substitute sex" out of loneliness. Do they have the deep connections they need to know they belong in God's family? Are the couples and families in your church making room for singles in their home lives?

Each person in your congregation or faith group who uses porn, no matter how much they use, does so for a reason. The road to wholeness and freedom begins with finding out their *why*.

HOW WELL DO YOU FOCUS ON THE REASONS DIFFERENT PEOPLE USE PORN AND TAILOR YOUR MINISTRY APPROACH ACCORDINGLY?

▶ **Q&A** WITH **MARK REGNERUS**

MARK REGNERUS
Professor, researcher and author

Mark Regnerus is an associate professor of sociology at the University of Texas at Austin and a faculty associate at the university's Population Research Center. His research is in the areas of sexual behavior, family and religion. Mark is the author of two books: *Premarital Sex in America: How Young Americans Meet, Mate, and Think about Marrying*, which describes the norms, behaviors and mating market realities facing young adults, and *Forbidden Fruit: Sex and Religion in the Lives of American Teenagers*, which tells the story of how religion does—and does not—shape teenagers' sexual decision-making. His work has been widely reviewed and his research and opinion pieces have been featured in numerous media outlets. Most recently, he was the author of a 2012 study appearing in *Social Science Research* on the comparatively optimal outcomes of young adults from stably married families.

Q: Some of your work focuses on "sexual economics," the social and relational impact of the cheapening of sex. How do you see porn fitting into that sociological framework?

A: Pornography and masturbation are nothing if not the "cheapest" forms of sex. But modern pornography is distinctive in that it not only *supplies* cheap sex but stimulates interest in it, too. That is not how supply-and-demand curves typically work. Instead, porn creates—then meets—demand with a near-infinite supply, kept afloat by its propensity toward compulsion. Even the market in prostitution does not function like that.

The second half of the 20th century birthed three forms of technology that function to drive down the "price" of sex. Fertility control and online pornography each, in their own way, seek to "free" sexual relationships—the Pill from unwanted pregnancies, and porn from the demands of self-control and the challenges that come from navigating relationships and the real-time wishes of real people. Throw in online dating-and-meeting software, which makes the process of accessing cheap sex more efficient, and you have the ingredients that have combined to bring us to this place.

The hook-up culture isn't just "out there" anymore. It's inside the Church: masked, moderated (a bit) and justified, prompting congregations everywhere to do soul searching over whether they're genuinely utilizing technology to better evangelize the world or, instead, to conform to it.

Q: Your book *Premarital Sex in America* examines the sex lives of young adults in the U.S. In your view, what role does porn play in young adults' sexual, social and relational decision-making?

A: It is difficult for those of us who grew up before the Internet to truly identify with how sexual education and assumptions about relationships have changed *because the Internet exists*. Women are entirely correct when they perceive that pornography creates competition. There may have been an era in which a man dabbling with porn would have had trouble retaining the sexual interest of a woman, but that era is no more. Women now consider it the new cost of doing business with men. To be sure, breaking off a relationship because of pornography use can be a rational and moral reaction—but few recognize that doing so also contributes to the broader retreat from marriage and significant relationships about which many of us claim to be concerned. Hence for both good and bad reasons, the flight from marriage in the Church continues unabated. This is the pornographic "double bind," wherein women find themselves stuck between unhappy scenarios—the unwanted porn use of the man they are with, the elevated odds of the same among the man they might leave him for, and the risk of being alone. On the matter of men and pornography, the data suggest you may not be able to flee far enough.

▶ Q&A WITH AUDREY ASSAD

AUDREY ASSAD
Songwriter and musician

Audrey Assad is the daughter of a Syrian refugee and an author, speaker, producer and critically lauded songwriter and musician. She releases music she calls "soundtracks for prayer" on the label Fortunate Fall Records, which she co-owns with her husband. Audrey has penned contemplative songs of worship for Matt Maher, Christy Nockels, Brett Younker, Sarah Hart, Meredith Andrews and others—her passion is to write fragrant, prayerful music that leads to encountering Jesus Christ, even in the silence of the heart.

www.AudreyAssad.com

Q: Barna found that teen girls and young women under 25 are three times as likely as women 25 and older to seek out porn at least once a month (33% vs. 11%). Yet there is still a persistent belief in the culture and in the Church that young women are not at risk of sexual addiction or even temptation in this area. What are your thoughts on this massive disparity between fact and assumption?

A: I have so many thoughts on this that it's difficult to organize them. But I'll say these two things: First, I think gender stereotypes run rampant inside Christianity. Femininity is traditionally associated with things like purity and modesty. Because of these stereotypes and how deeply they are ingrained in the Church, women do not feel free to confess or speak publicly about lust, sexual addictions, pornography, masturbation or anything of the sort. This perpetuates a cycle of shame and bondage and silence for the women who are affected, and in turn reinforces the erroneous idea that women do not struggle with things like this—the idea that it's a "guy problem" remains the status quo because women do not feel safe to speak—they feel they will not be seen as feminine or womanly.

Second, the disparity has to be due in part to the fact that Christian teaching in youth ministry has barely shifted in all these years to reflect what the newest studies show. Young girls go to retreats and camps all over this country and hear that pornography addiction is an issue that affects men. Again, this reinforces the idea in their minds that they cannot tell anyone about their struggles with pornography, and perpetuates the cycle of shame and bondage and silence.

Q: What changes would you like to see in how the Church talks about and handles sex addiction, particularly among women, but more generally as well?

A: I would love to see pornography addiction de-stigmatized and stripped of any unnecessary stereotyping in terms of gender. I personally believe that pornography addiction is proof of humanity's search for God (just as, arguably, all sin is). If Christians stop treating it like a secret to be ashamed of and begin to confront and confess it honestly, dig down to the roots of it, and proactively address the heart issues underneath it, I think real progress could be made.

I also would love to see the Church arming young people with knowledge about pornography addiction. I personally encountered it at 15 years old, and had no language or framework within which to contextualize what I was seeing—I had really never even heard of porn. The first time I heard about it in a church setting, it was a Sunday School course that focused mainly on men, their biology and their potential weaknesses. It warned that all serial killers interviewed on the subject were addicted to hardcore porn. You can imagine how that made me feel as a 15-year-old female pornography addict, and I can tell you with certainty how it did *not* make me feel. It did not make me feel safe or welcome to speak out loud what I was struggling with in private. I only felt shame and a deep, growing reticence to ever inform anyone of my addiction because I felt certain I was a freak and not "feminine" enough.

Q: Looking at the Barna findings, what (if anything) stands out to you as encouraging, and why? What (if anything) do you find discouraging, and why?

A: I find it somewhat encouraging that young people consider more types of images to be pornography than do older adults. That sensitivity is potentially good, in my opinion—in a person who wants to avoid pornography (the sort of person some of these young people may eventually become), a sensitive conscience and nuanced "porn detection" sensor is incredibly helpful.

I find it simultaneously encouraging and discouraging—if that is possible—that young people are so likely to see pornography as good. I hate to see body positivity (which is good) and gender equality (also good) spin off into thinking that keeps people in bondage. But I also affirm and celebrate the fact that some of today's young people do not carry the same crippling shame about sex and sexuality that I did at their age. I have undergone more therapy because of my sexual baggage from fundamentalist Christianity than because of pornography addiction. Perhaps today's young people, when well informed and instructed on the matter of pornography, will find more freedom more quickly than I did because they are less encumbered by shame. I have no way of knowing if that's true, but I hope it will be.

50 SHADES OF WRONG

Half of all Americans say porn is bad for society … but some kinds of porn are worse than others.

YOUNG ADULTS USE MORE PORN—AND ARE LESS LIKELY TO SAY IT'S BAD FOR SOCIETY

● ● ● Very bad   ● ● ● Somewhat bad

AGE

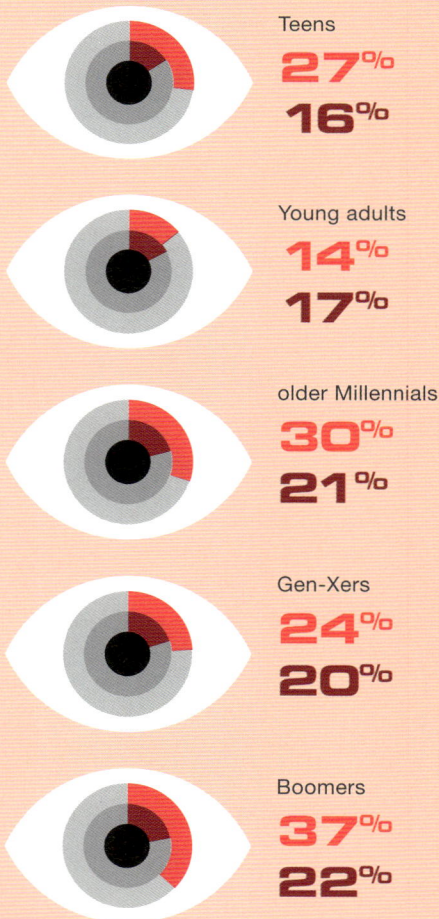

Teens
27%
16%

Young adults
14%
17%

older Millennials
30%
21%

Gen-Xers
24%
20%

Boomers
37%
22%

GENDER

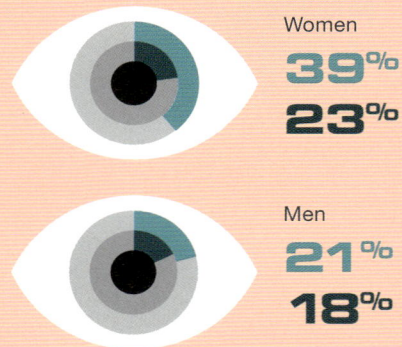

Women
39%
23%

Men
21%
18%

FAITH PRACTICE

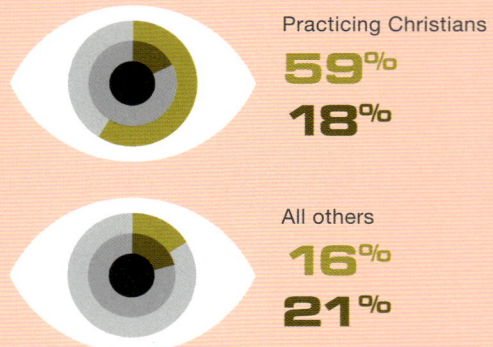

Practicing Christians
59%
18%

All others
16%
21%

MOST PEOPLE AGREE THAT SOME TYPES OF PORN ARE ALWAYS WRONG

Porn users who think porn that depicts any of the following is always wrong:

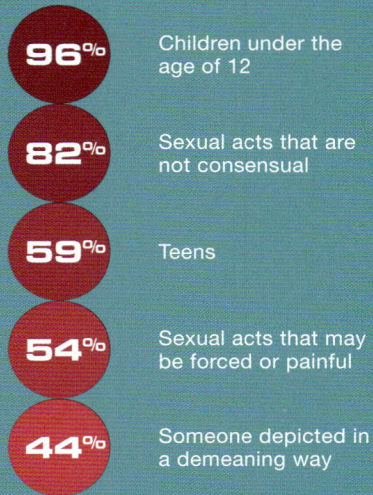

96% Children under the age of 12

82% Sexual acts that are not consensual

59% Teens

54% Sexual acts that may be forced or painful

44% Someone depicted in a demeaning way

BUT THE MORE YOU USE PORN, THE LESS WRONG YOU THINK IT IS

Regular porn viewers who think porn that depicts any of the following is always wrong:

- ● Daily users
- ● Weekly users
- ● Monthly users

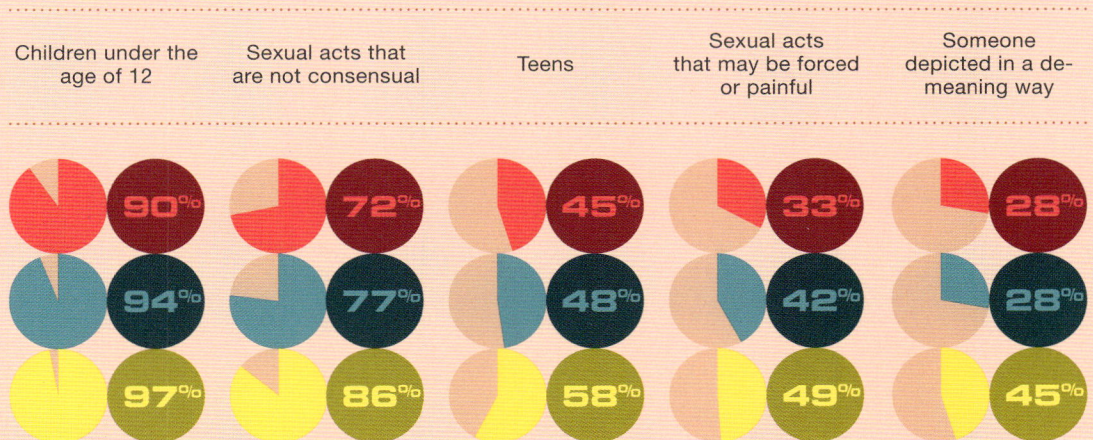

Children under the age of 12	Sexual acts that are not consensual	Teens	Sexual acts that may be forced or painful	Someone depicted in a demeaning way
90%	72%	45%	33%	28%
94%	77%	48%	42%	28%
97%	86%	58%	49%	45%

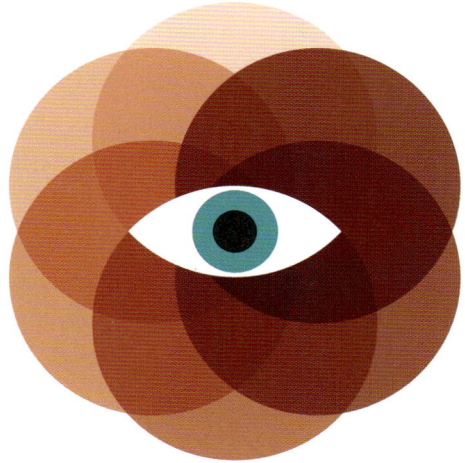

3.

PORN & MORALITY

Freedom of conscience, enshrined in the First Amendment to the U.S. Constitution, is deeply rooted in the nation's DNA. The earliest colonists left Europe in search of religious freedom and their descendants codified protections against religious tyranny in the country's founding documents.

Americans cherish the right to believe whatever they wish—which turns out to be a mixed blessing. For example, reaching consensus around a moral code for society is difficult when no one can agree on the source or arbiter of that code.

Most of our cultural forebears looked to a higher being as the ultimate source of moral knowledge and the final moral authority. But recent Barna research shows that today's Americans are more prone to turn inward for such knowledge. Half of all U.S. adults believe that "ethics and morals are based on what seems right to a person based on their own judgment and ideas" (53%). Nine out of 10 believe "people should not criticize someone else's life choices" (89%) and eight out of 10 say "people can believe whatever they want, as long as those beliefs don't affect society" (79%). This inward-oriented search for truth or purpose also leads nine out of 10 adults to agree "the best way to find yourself is by looking within yourself" (91%) and 86 percent to say "to be fulfilled in life, you should pursue

THE ONLY MORAL CODE MOST PEOPLE AGREE ON IS THAT EACH PERSON IS THE SOLE MORAL AUTHORITY FOR HIMSELF

"These days people turn inward for moral reassurance rather than outward to public moral standards." Could this actually be an opportunity for the Church? Jesus taught that our morality works from the inside out (compare Matt. 6:1–8 and 15:11, 17–20). By fighting for external moral standards, has our message become confused? Could we regain a hearing for Christian morality by drawing on Jesus' teaching?

the things you desire the most." When it comes to the sexual expression of that desire, nearly nine out of 10 Americans believe "each person has to decide his or her own sexual boundaries" (88%).

In other words, the only moral code most people agree on is that each person is the sole moral authority for himself. Each individual must decide for himself what is right and wrong, taking into account his needs, desires, hopes and dreams. In their book *Good Faith,* David Kinnaman and Gabe Lyons call this the *morality of self-fulfillment.*[34]

Accounting for society's allegiance to this moral code is essential for understanding attitudes toward pornography in the U.S. today. Not only is there a lack of consensus on the moral goodness or badness of porn, but there are also myriad views about its impact on society. These are largely based on how porn is perceived to be or not to be a source of self-fulfillment—because self-fulfillment is the final word on morality in today's culture.

Keeping in mind the underlying assumption that self-fulfillment is a moral nonnegotiable, let's take a look at how U.S. teens and adults view the morality of porn.

PORN ON THE SCALES OF MORALITY

Teens, young adults and adults 25 and older rated a series of action statements according to a five-point scale: "always OK," "usually OK," "neither wrong nor OK," "usually wrong" and "always wrong." Combining the percentages of those who chose always and usually wrong for each statement, a picture emerges of where using porn ranks on a list of possible immoral actions.

The short answer? Low.

Barely half of adults say viewing porn is wrong (54%) and it ranks only seventh on a list of 11 actions—behind overeating (58%), which is #4.

ACTIONS THAT ARE WRONG: ADULTS 25+

base: adults 25 and older	% usually + always wrong
1. taking something that belongs to someone else	95
2. having a romantic relationship with someone other than a spouse	89
3. saying something that isn't true	87
4. overeating	58
5. wanting something that belongs to someone else	57
6. thinking negatively about someone with a different point of view	55
7. viewing pornographic images	54
8. reading erotic or pornographic content (no pictures)	46
9. not recycling	44
10. significant consumption of electricity or water	39
11. watching sexually explicit scenes on TV or in a movie	37

55% of adults 25+ say viewing porn is wrong

Teens and young adults are roughly 10 points less likely than older adults to think each of the actions is wrong. In addition, the ranking order below the top three are quite different between the younger and older age cohorts. (It is not necessarily surprising that the two groups agree on these top three actions as always or usually wrong, since these top three are the most likely to affect someone else negatively. Whereas the remaining items are all primarily questions of personal or internal morality. An exception might be "not recycling," which may explain why teens and young adults rank it higher.)

Actions that may negatively impact the environment rank higher among teens and young adults than among older adults. The younger group has grown up in the age of climate change, manmade natural disasters, droughts, mandatory recycling, electric cars, pesticide-free farming and so on. Thus it is not surprising that they perceive a moral dimension to actions with environmental implications. (It is notable, however, that "not recycling" ranks so highly.)

32% of teens and young adults say viewing porn is wrong

ACTIONS THAT ARE WRONG: TEENS & YOUNG ADULTS 13 TO 24

base: teens and young adults 13–24	% usually + always wrong
1. taking something that belongs to someone else	88
2. having a romantic relationship with someone other than a spouse	75
3. saying something that isn't true	71
4. not recycling	56
5. thinking negatively about someone with a different point of view	55
6. overeating	48
7. significant consumption of electricity or water	38
8. wanting something that belongs to someone else	32
9. viewing pornographic images	32
10. reading erotic or pornographic content (no pictures)	27
11. watching sexually explicit scenes on TV or in a movie	24

Older adults seem to retain a greater vestige of Judeo-Christian morality than younger Americans. For example, "overeating" (58%) and "wanting something that belongs to someone else" (57%) are both sins according to Christian tradition: gluttony and covetousness. Nearly six in 10 adults 25 and older say these actions are immoral, compared to just half of teens and young adults who say overeating is wrong (48%) and one-third who believe coveting is wrong (32%).

The moral code of self-fulfillment is alive and well in both age groups. "Thinking negatively about someone with a different point of view" is perceived to be always or usually wrong by more than half of teens and young adults (55%) and adults 25 and older (55%). The highest moral good is not figuring out what is right, but accepting each person's view as "right for them."

For most teens and young adults, using porn seems to fall into this category. Only one-third believes viewing pornographic images is always or usually wrong (32%), compared to more than half of older adults (54%). About one-quarter says reading erotic content (27%) or watching sexually explicit TV or movie scenes (24%) is immoral.

There appears to be a momentous generational shift underway in how pornography is perceived, morally speaking, within our culture—at least when it comes to each person choosing for himself whether to use porn. Yet when it comes to assessing porn's impact on society more broadly, people are more apt to hold a negative view.

Which presents an interesting paradox of belief: Porn is fine for individuals but bad for society.

THERE APPEARS TO BE A MOMENTOUS GENERATIONAL SHIFT UNDERWAY IN HOW PORNOGRAPHY IS PERCEIVED WITHIN OUR CULTURE

BAD PORN

Half of the U.S. population ages 13 and older say porn is bad for society (50%). About two in five say it's neither bad nor good (39%) and the remaining 11 percent believe porn is good for society, overall.

PORN IS BAD FOR SOCIETY, BY AGE

% among U.S. teens, young adults and adults 25+

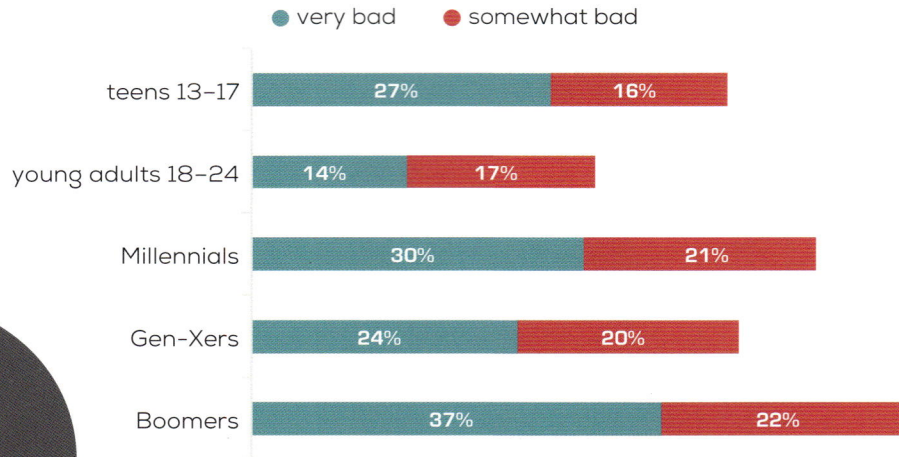

● very bad   ● somewhat bad

	very bad	somewhat bad
teens 13–17	27%	16%
young adults 18–24	14%	17%
Millennials	30%	21%
Gen-Xers	24%	20%
Boomers	37%	22%

31%
of young adults say porn is bad for society

Perhaps surprisingly, older Millennials (25 to 30) are more likely than their older and younger counterparts to say porn is *very* bad for society (30%, compared to 24% Gen-Xers and 14% young adults 18 to 24). The reasons for the significant difference between older and younger Millennials are difficult to pin down, but it could indicate a tipping point some twentysomethings experience after having used porn for a number of years, or after having suffered negative repercussions of their partner's porn use. It may be that younger adults haven't yet experienced many negative consequences related to porn. When they reach their late 20s, serious relationships or marriage are more likely to be part of the equation and the relational impacts of porn may be felt more acutely.

Alternatively, the difference between younger and older Millennials may infer a considerable shift in wider cultural paradigms about pornography. Teens' perceptions of porn's impact on society seem to contradict this theory, however. Forty-three percent of 13- to 17-year-olds believe porn is bad for society, compared to only 31 percent of 18- to 24-year-olds.

PORN IS BAD FOR SOCIETY, BY MARITAL STATUS

% among U.S. adults 25+

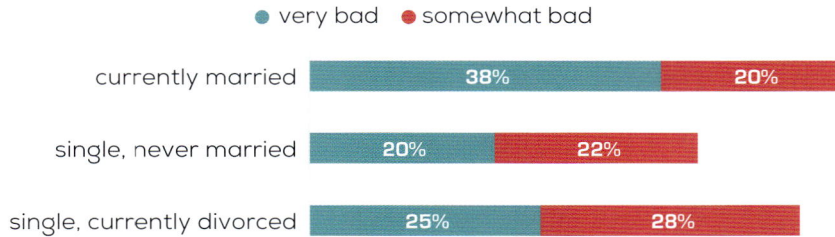

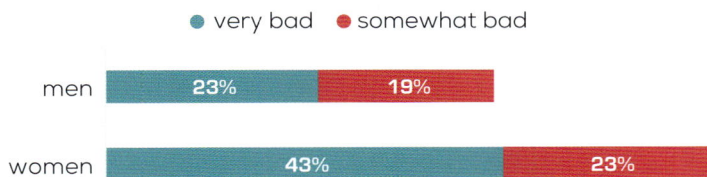

● very bad   ● somewhat bad

	very bad	somewhat bad
currently married	38%	20%
single, never married	20%	22%
single, currently divorced	25%	28%

Among the general population 25 and older, there is a significant difference between married and single (that is, divorced and never married) adults in their views on porn's impact on society. Singles are much less likely to think that porn is bad in this regard. While nearly six in 10 marrieds (58%) think porn is very or somewhat bad for society, just 47 percent of all singles agree.

Marriage seems to have a lasting influence on a person's views, even if he or she is no longer married: Divorced adults (53%) are more likely than those who have never been married (42%) to say porn has a negative impact on society. (It's likely that some of these divorced Americans directly experienced porn's relational destructiveness—explored further in the next chapter—but how many and in what ways are questions beyond the scope of this study.)

In general people find thinking negatively about someone else as morally worse than using pornography, and young people rank not recycling and conspicuous consumption of electricity or water as morally worse. What does this say about what we value as a society? How can the Church lead the way in reordering our priorities?

PORN IS BAD FOR SOCIETY, BY GENDER

% among U.S. adults 25+

● very bad   ● somewhat bad

	very bad	somewhat bad
men	23%	19%
women	43%	23%

As previously discussed, women are less likely than men to view porn. They are also far more likely to believe porn is bad for society (66% vs. 42% of men), and less likely to be neutral on its effects (29% vs. 46%) or to say porn's impact is a net good for society (5% vs. 12%).

The greatest difference between people on this question is not gender, however; it is between practicing Christians and all others. Three-quarters of practicing Christians (77%) say porn is bad for society—six in 10 say it is very bad (59%)—compared to about one-third of all other Americans 13 and older (37%). Half of the general population that does not practice Christianity says porn is neither good nor bad for society (49%), contrasted with one in five practicing Christians who is neutral on porn's societal effects (19%). And those who do not practice Christianity are four times more likely than practicing Christians to say porn is good for society overall (14% vs. 3%).

PORN IS BAD FOR SOCIETY, BY PRACTICING FAITH

% among U.S. teens, young adults and adults 25+

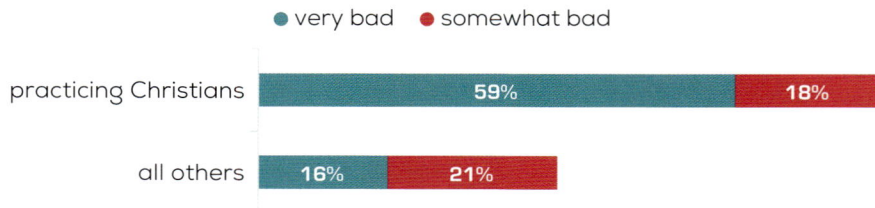

● very bad   ● somewhat bad

practicing Christians	59%	18%
all others	16%	21%

About one in 10 among all Americans say porn is, on balance, a good thing for society (11%). Even these teens and adults, however, draw the line at certain types of pornographic content. Nearly all Americans who use porn say images that include children under the age of 12 are wrong (97%), and nine out of 10 say images that depict non-consensual sex (i.e., rape) are wrong (89%). Much smaller percentages disapprove of gay porn (28%) or of porn that includes more than two people at once (25%).

SEXUAL IMAGES THAT ARE WRONG

	% wrong	% okay	% not sure
base: U.S. teens and adults 13 and older who actively seek out porn			
children under the age of 12	97	1	1
sexual acts that are not consensual	89	6	4
sexual acts that may be forced or painful	79	10	11
teens	76	12	11
someone depicted in a demeaning way	69	15	16
sexual acts between two people of the same gender	28	56	16
sexual acts involving more than two people at once	25	60	16

PORN USE AND GUILT

Sociopaths aside, human beings tend to feel uncomfortable when they do something they believe is wrong. Acting contrary to one's convictions usually causes stress to the human psyche. And often those feelings of stress are the result of guilt—an emotional experience that occurs when a person realizes she has violated a moral standard.

The connection between discomfort and guilt led researchers to ask those who use porn how comfortable they feel with the amount they use. Their level of discomfort could indicate guilt-induced stress related to porn use.

By segmenting porn users by how often they report seeking out porn, Barna found that more frequent porn use correlates to higher levels of comfort related to porn use. In other words, if you use porn often, you're more likely to feel okay about it. If you use porn less often, you're more likely to feel uncomfortable with it. Eighty-nine percent of daily porn users, 77 percent of weekly porn users, 70 percent of once-or-twice-a-month porn users and 52 percent of those who use porn less often are comfortable with how much porn they use. And those who seek out porn less than monthly are *more than 10 times more likely* than those who do so daily to say they would rather not use porn at all (36% vs. 3%).

Those who use porn most frequently are most comfortable with how much they use

HOW COMFORTABLE PEOPLE FEEL WITH THEIR USE OF PORN, BY FREQUENCY OF USE

	% daily	% weekly	% once or twice a month	% less often
base: teens and adults 13 and older who actively seek out porn				
I am comfortable with how much porn I use	89	77	70	52
I would rather not use it as much as I do, but some is OK	8	17	19	12
I would rather not use porn at all	3	7	12	36

The dynamic between porn use and discomfort is a kind of chicken-and-egg question: Do those most predisposed to guilt about porn limit their porn use, or does using porn more frequently lead to less mental stress associated with guilt? It may be that both are true to some extent.

Compared to older age groups, fewer teens who seek out porn report being comfortable with the amount of porn they use (52%

vs. ~69%). Roughly equal proportions say they wish they used less (25%) or none at all (22%).

Among twentysomethings who are not comfortable with their use of porn, it is more common to wish they used less than to say they would like to stop altogether. But among Gen-Xers and Boomers, the opposite is true: Those who are uncomfortable with how much porn they use are more likely to say they would rather not use porn at all.

IF YOU USE PORN OFTEN, YOU'RE MORE LIKELY TO FEEL OKAY ABOUT IT. IF YOU USE PORN LESS OFTEN, YOU'RE MORE LIKELY TO FEEL UNCOMFORTABLE WITH IT

HOW COMFORTABLE PEOPLE FEEL WITH THEIR USE OF PORN, BY GENERATION

base: teens and adults 13 and older who actively seek out porn	% teens 13–17	% young adults 18–24	% Millennials 25–30	% Gen-Xers 31–50	% Boomers 51–69
I am comfortable with how much porn I use	52	68	69	72	64
I would rather not use it as much as I do, but some is OK	25	22	19	10	12
I would rather not use porn at all	22	10	13	18	24

Predictably, practicing Christians who seek out porn at least on occasion are much less comfortable than others with their use of porn. About two in five say they are comfortable (39%), compared to nearly three-quarters of teens and adults who are not practicing Christians (73%). They are also about twice as likely to say they'd like to stop (40%) than to say they'd like to use less (21%). Teens and adults who do not practice Christianity are equally likely to say they want to use porn less (13%) or to stop (14%).

HOW COMFORTABLE PEOPLE FEEL WITH THEIR USE OF PORN, BY PRACTICING FAITH

	% practicing Christians	% all others
base: teens and adults 13 and older who actively seek out porn		
I am comfortable with how much porn I use	39	73
I would rather not use it as much as I do, but some is OK	21	13
I would rather not use porn at all	40	14

GOOD PORN?

PRO-PORN ACTIVISTS ARGUE THAT PORNOGRAPHY IS EMPOWERING FOR WOMEN, USEFUL FOR SEX EDUCATION AND ULTIMATELY VALUABLE FOR SOCIETY

The data on practicing Christians' views and feelings support what is likely an assumption held by many readers: Christians, by and large, believe pornography is immoral. Yet traditional Judeo-Christian morals are not the only word in the cultural conversation surrounding porn. Pro-porn activists argue that pornography is empowering for women, useful for sex education and ultimately valuable for society.

Let's examine the evidence for these claims. (In chapter 4, we'll look at the counterarguments.)

Empowerment

Sex-positive feminism arose in what has been called the "sex wars" of the 1980s to counter the claims of anti-porn feminists who place pornography at the center of the battle against oppression for women. For those in the sex-positive camp, sexual freedom is an essential component of women's equality. As such, sex-positive feminists oppose legal or social efforts to control sexual activities between consenting adults. Pornography is simply one expression of liberated sexuality.

"The popular rhetoric about pornography as violent, degrading, and harmful to women and society," writes scholar Mireille Miller-Young, "ignores the diverse ways that women actually interact with it. . . . . Women enter the pornography industry because they are enthusiastic about its potential for lucrative, flexible and independent work."[35]

> Coming from more traditional sectors like nursing and retail, women found that pornography offered them greater control of their labor, and surprisingly, it treated them with more humanity. Some women found that it enabled them to rise out of poverty, take care of their families or go to college. Others emphasize the creative aspects of pornography, and say it allows them to increase their economic mobility while also making a bold statement about female pleasure.[36]

According to this argument, porn is empowering because the performers are using their sexuality to their own ends, to make money and support themselves.[37] If the Christian community is perceived as pitted against the equality and empowerment of women, our arguments against porn use are unlikely to gain traction.

Sex Education

A leading sexologist in Denmark has called for pornography to be shown in the classroom, claiming that starting a debate about the industry could help teenagers become "conscientious and critical

IF THE CHRISTIAN COMMUNITY IS PERCEIVED AS PITTED AGAINST THE EMPOWERMENT OF WOMEN, OUR ARGUMENTS AGAINST PORN ARE UNLIKELY TO GAIN TRACTION

consumers" who are able to tell the difference between pornography and the reality of sexual relationships. "We want our kids to have exciting and gratifying sex lives, so an open-minded, constructive dialogue is the best way to make sure that they are able to make meaningful decisions for themselves."[38]

An op-ed in *The Guardian* recently took up the argument:

> It's time we wake up to the fact that a sex education curriculum that does not include porn is not a sex education curriculum, and furthermore is one that is failing in its safeguarding duty. Because better discussion of porn and consent is vital when set against a backdrop of child sexual exploitation. Teenagers have passionate views on sex and porn and want to talk about them. Embarrassing though it may be, it's high time adults started talking back.[39]

If nothing else, proponents say, sex education that includes porn provides an alternative narrative to the violence, racism and sexism endemic to hardcore pornography, and can teach young people how to think critically about the sexually explicit media they consume. Rather than seeking to prohibit sex education altogether, the Christian community might consider how to provide an alternative narrative about sexuality overall and teach young people to think critically about society's underlying assumptions about sex.

THE CHRISTIAN COMMUNITY MIGHT TEACH YOUNG PEOPLE TO THINK CRITICALLY ABOUT SOCIETY'S UNDERLYING ASSUMPTIONS ABOUT SEX

Positive Impact

In at least one scientific study, viewing porn was found to help limit the brain's production of the hormone cortisol, which is associated with stress. Men who viewed erotic images performed nearly 50 percent better than those who didn't on the math portion of a stress test.[40] Even if this is not a convincing argument in favor of porn use, it may explain one aspect of porn's appeal: as a reliable stress-reliever.

More compelling and harder to refute is data that shows a correlation between greater access to porn and lower rates of sex crimes, including exhibitionism, rape and child abuse. Across the world, as men gain more access to Internet erotica, sex crimes go down. The argument here is that porn provides a net positive value to society by offering an avenue of sexual release to those who might otherwise commit crimes against the most vulnerable, including women and children.[41]

Finally, there are some who argue that porn is an important component of "sex positivity," which seeks to countermand messages and attitudes about sex that are based on shame. The sex-positive movement is gaining cultural ground: Two in five adults 18 and older agree that "sexual images and situations in media are important for showing people how to be positive about sex" (42%).

Insofar as Christians rely on shame-based arguments against porn use, we may find it increasingly difficult to gain a hearing in the wider culture as sex-positive views proliferate. The sex-positive message aligns seamlessly with the morality of self-fulfillment, and is thus more culturally resonant than traditional Judeo-Christian morals—especially when those morals are presented in terms of shame and guilt, rather than in terms of God's good intentions for human flourishing. But as we'll see in the next chapter, though the research does not show direct, sole causation when it comes to porn use and sexual violence, there are certainly reasons to believe porn contributes to, and is implicated in, the prevalence of sexual violence.

INSOFAR AS CHRISTIANS RELY ON SHAME-BASED ARGUMENTS AGAINST PORN, WE MAY FIND IT INCREASINGLY DIFFICULT TO GAIN A HEARING IN THE WIDER CULTURE

▶ Q&A WITH JOEL HESCH

JOEL HESCH

Author and founder of Proven Men Ministries

Joel Hesch is an author and founder of Proven Men Ministries, a nonprofit organization dedicated to restoring families and helping men break free from porn and sex addiction. After breaking free from his own 20-year addiction, Joel created "the proven path for sexual integrity." His vision is to help 1 million people experience victory from strongholds of porn and sex addition.

www.ProvenMen.org

Q: The groups and materials from Proven Men, the ministry you started 15 years ago, emphasize what you call "heartwork," a shift of internal desires, rather than behavior modification. Why do you think this is important? In your experience, what are the most common "internal desires" that need to be reoriented?

A: What we refer to as "heartwork" is vital to experiencing victory from bondage to porn. People don't break free from an addiction to porn or sex by setting boundaries or following rules, because those things do nothing to address the internal sensual desires that lead to chasing after porn. Proven Men focuses on creating an internal heart shift that produces a longing to live out an overall "proven" life. We call our 12-week study "heartwork" because it goes after a man's heart through daily reflection and time with God.

Porn isn't the real problem—lust is. Unbridled lust is what fuels a desire to look at porn or engage in sexual fantasy. But there is yet a deeper issue that feeds lust: pride and selfishness. That's where the battle must be fought and won. These twin sins of pride and selfishness cause a man to become so consumed with his rights that he loses sight of the real prize of true intimacy with God or a spouse. As long as selfishness and pride dominate, he will always be a slave to some form of sexual integrity issue and countless other self-motivated sins like greed and anger. Only when he gets serious about dying to selfishness and pride will his heart be ready to pursue and enjoy things that are healthy and pure.

Q: Proven Men focuses on helping men who have already fallen prey to porn. Do you have ideas about how to keep young men and teen boys from the disordered internal desires that lead to porn use? Can "heartwork" be a prevention as well as a cure? And if so, how?

A: One of the biggest lies to single men is that their struggle with porn or sexual integrity will go away when they get married. Patterns developed as a single carry over into marriage. I personally know how defeating it is to get married and then realize that the addiction is growing. On my seventh wedding anniversary I confessed to my wife that not only did I still struggle with porn and sex addiction, but I had crossed another line by asking a woman from church to go to bed with me to fulfill one of my many fantasies. That's why I am passionate about telling teens and young adults to do business with it now, before they get married.

Half the men we have worked with over the past 15 years are single. The key for them is to use our materials to lay a strong foundation that must then be built on as they keep growing in faith and maturity. That means keeping other men active in their life for accountability and encouragement.

With respect to children and teens, the most important preventative measure is open and honest communication with a parent. Most of the men we work with tell us their dads either never talked with them about sex or discussed it only once. But kids need regular, open discussions with a parent about the things they struggle with and wonder about. If a parent isn't the source of wisdom, encouragement and guidance, then culture and their peers will be their main sources of information.

Children and teens also need parents who set boundaries. This might include installing an Internet filter; prohibiting smartphones, tablets or computers in bedrooms; setting curfews for being home; and turning off cell phones at a certain time at night. Parents should even consider granting themselves access to their kids' Facebook and Instagram accounts and buying monitoring software that allows them to read texts and emails.

The point is, parents need to build and maintain relationships so kids know their parents have their best interests at heart—even if they disagree with the boundaries.

SPECIAL REPORT
PASTORS & PORN

When they think about U.S. Protestant pastors as a group, nearly two-thirds of the pastors Barna interviewed say porn use is a major (6%) or significant (58%) problem among these leaders—but it's not the most pressing problem. About three-quarters say burnout (79%), marital problems (78%) or pride (73%) are bigger problems than porn use, and two-thirds say finances (65%) and disagreements among the church leadership (64%) outweigh porn as difficult issues pastors are dealing with.

Rather than only asking pastors about "pastors" as a macro group, researchers also asked church leaders about themselves. (All surveys were anonymous.) One in five youth pastors (21%) and one in seven senior pastors (14%) admitted they currently use porn. About half do so at least a few times per month, and the vast majority feels guilt or shame when they do so. More than half of youth pastors who use porn (56%) and one-third of senior pastors who use porn (33%) believe they are addicted.

Porn use by any church leader is a problem, but senior pastors' responses are cause for particular concern. Senior leaders are more likely than their youth leader counterparts to say that their job makes it easy to use porn in secret and that neither their spouse nor even a trusted friend is aware of their struggle. There also seems to be a tendency among senior leaders to underestimate or downplay the impact of porn use both on their ministry and on their relationships. And although a majority says they feel guilt or shame related to their porn use, senior pastors are less likely than youth leaders to say so.

These data combine to paint a portrait of senior leaders in isolation, too many of them unaware of or in denial about the spiritual and relational risks they are running—risks that have the potential to harm not only themselves but others. In recent years we have seen ample evidence that, for some pastors and priests, the spiritual power they wield can too easily lead to sexual coercion and abuse. If, as some experts suggest, porn is implicated in sexual violence, the Christian community and its leaders must bring these struggles into the light.

---

1 in 5 youth pastors

and **1 in 7 senior pastors use porn.**

That's more than 50,000 U.S. church leaders.

A high percentage of pastors (14%) and an even higher percentage of youth pastors (21%) admit they use porn on a regular basis. The research indicates that the isolated nature of ministry is a key factor. Pastors and churches build the isolation together. All too often, pastors fear honesty and congregations fear their pastor's vulnerability. How can churches become safe places for pastors to come out of isolation and into gracious accountability?

ALL PASTORS AND YOUTH PASTORS

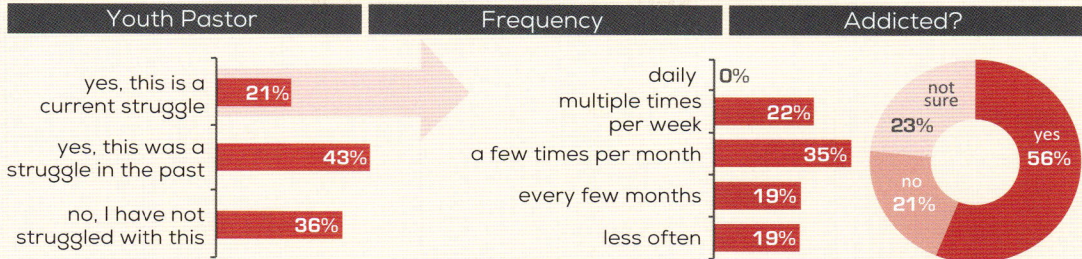

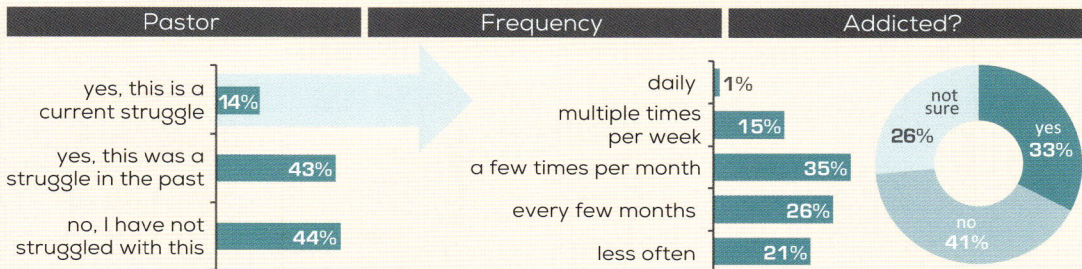

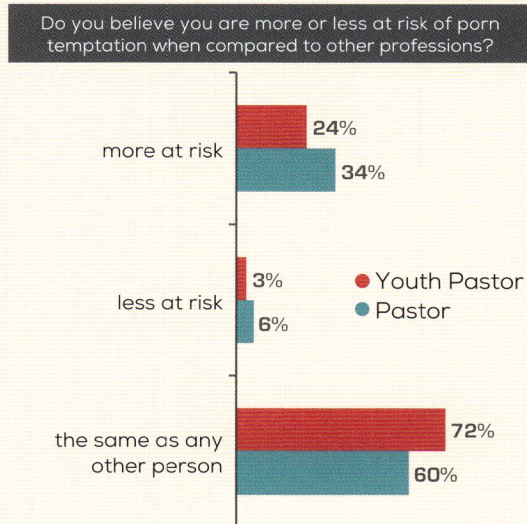

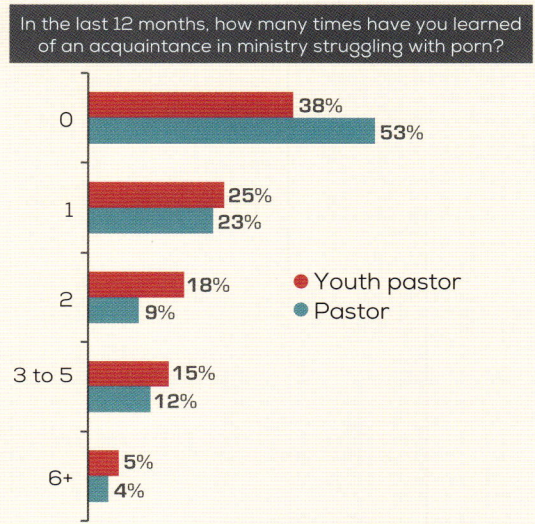

Youth Pastor | Frequency | Addicted?

Youth Pastor		Frequency	
yes, this is a current struggle	21%	daily	0%
yes, this was a struggle in the past	43%	multiple times per week	22%
no, I have not struggled with this	36%	a few times per month	35%
		every few months	19%
		less often	19%

Addicted?
- yes 56%
- no 21%
- not sure 23%

Pastor | Frequency | Addicted?

Pastor		Frequency	
yes, this is a current struggle	14%	daily	1%
yes, this was a struggle in the past	43%	multiple times per week	15%
no, I have not struggled with this	44%	a few times per month	35%
		every few months	26%
		less often	21%

Addicted?
- yes 33%
- no 41%
- not sure 26%

Do you believe you are more or less at risk of porn temptation when compared to other professions?

	Youth Pastor	Pastor
more at risk	24%	34%
less at risk	3%	6%
the same as any other person	72%	60%

In the last 12 months, how many times have you learned of an acquaintance in ministry struggling with porn?

	Youth pastor	Pastor
0	38%	53%
1	25%	23%
2	18%	9%
3 to 5	15%	12%
6+	5%	4%

PASTORS AND YOUTH PASTORS WHO CURRENTLY USE PORN

View on Porn

● ● I feel a sense of guilt when I use porn   ● ● It doesn't really bother me to use it

Youth pastor — 94% | 1%
Pastor — 86% | 5%

History & Avenues

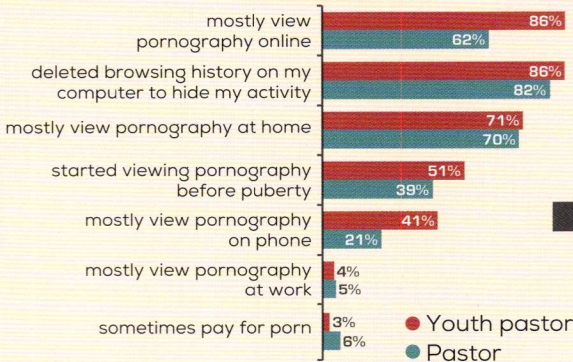

● Youth pastor
● Pastor

mostly view pornography online — 86% / 62%
deleted browsing history on my computer to hide my activity — 86% / 82%
mostly view pornography at home — 71% / 70%
started viewing pornography before puberty — 51% / 39%
mostly view pornography on phone — 41% / 21%
mostly view pornography at work — 4% / 5%
sometimes pay for porn — 3% / 6%

Effects of Porn

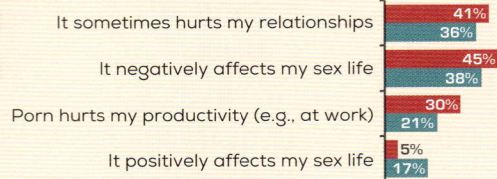

It sometimes hurts my relationships — 41% / 36%
It negatively affects my sex life — 45% / 38%
Porn hurts my productivity (e.g., at work) — 30% / 21%
It positively affects my sex life — 5% / 17%

Stop Use

I am currently trying to stop using porn — 83% / 71%
I have tried to stop using it, but have been unable to (or started again) — 68% / 54%

The nature of my job makes it easier to use pornography secretly

● ● very true   ● ● somewhat true   ● ● not really true   ● ● not at all true

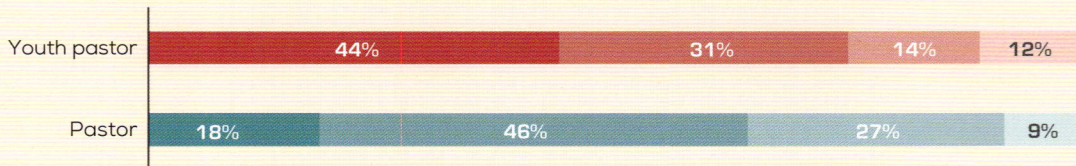

Youth pastor — 7% | 12% | 27% | 55%
Pastor — 9% | 30% | 20% | 41%

The use of porn negatively impacted my ministry

● ● very true   ● ● somewhat true   ● ● not really true   ● ● not at all true

Youth pastor — 44% | 31% | 14% | 12%
Pastor — 18% | 46% | 27% | 9%

Pastors Who Use Porn Feel . . .

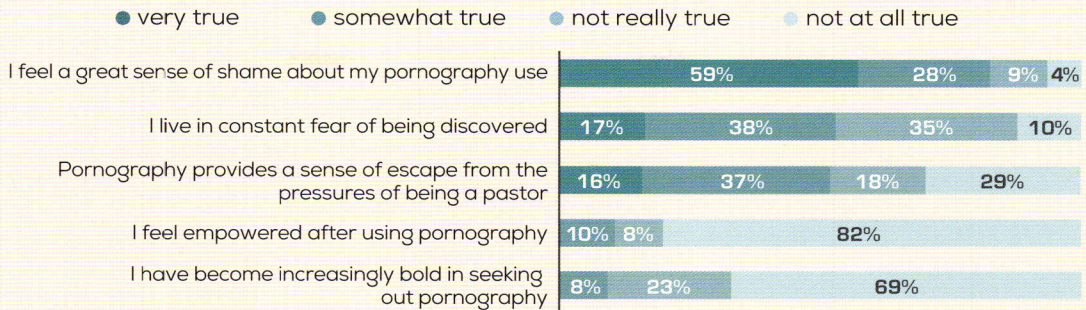

● very true ● somewhat true ● not really true ● not at all true

	very true	somewhat true	not really true	not at all true
I feel a great sense of shame about my pornography use	59%	28%	9%	4%
I live in constant fear of being discovered	17%	38%	35%	10%
Pornography provides a sense of escape from the pressures of being a pastor	16%	37%	18%	29%
I feel empowered after using pornography	10%	8%	82%	
I have become increasingly bold in seeking out pornography	8%	23%	69%	

Who knows about your porn use?

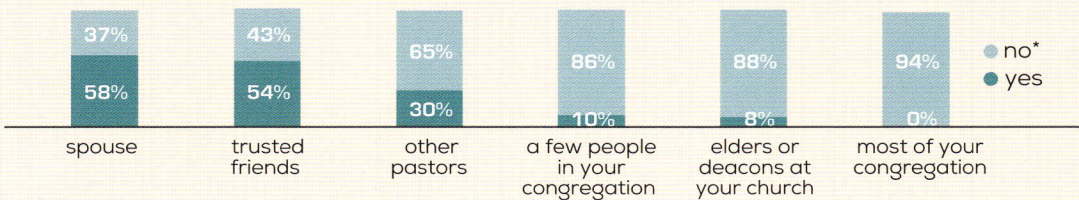

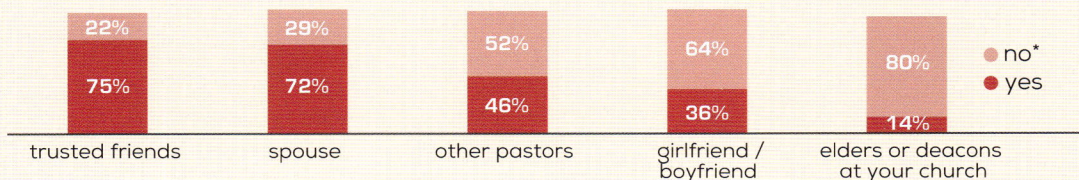

● no* ● yes

	spouse	trusted friends	other pastors	a few people in your congregation	elders or deacons at your church	most of your congregation
no*	37%	43%	65%	86%	88%	94%
yes	58%	54%	30%	10%	8%	0%

Youth Pastors Who Use Porn Feel . . .

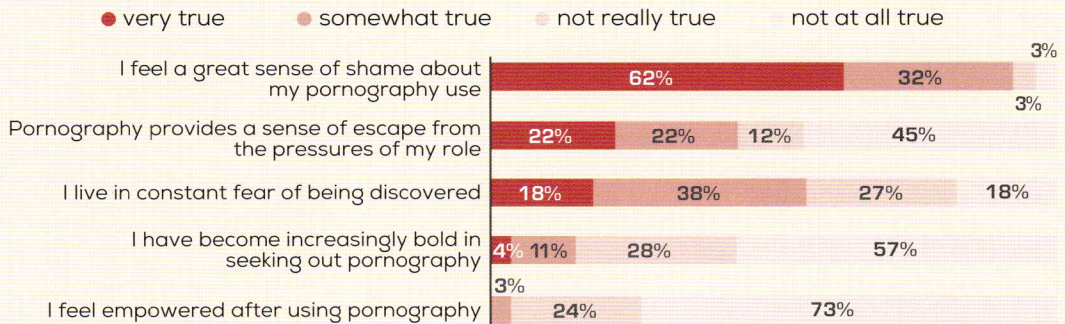

● very true ● somewhat true ● not really true ● not at all true

	very true	somewhat true	not really true	not at all true
I feel a great sense of shame about my pornography use	62%	32%	3%	3%
Pornography provides a sense of escape from the pressures of my role	22%	22%	12%	45%
I live in constant fear of being discovered	18%	38%	27%	18%
I have become increasingly bold in seeking out pornography	4%	11%	28%	57%
I feel empowered after using pornography	3%	24%	73%	

Who knows about your porn use?

● no* ● yes

	trusted friends	spouse	other pastors	girlfriend / boyfriend	elders or deacons at your church
no*	22%	29%	52%	64%	80%
yes	75%	72%	46%	36%	14%

*The third option was "not sure."

IF PORN IS WRONG, HOW WRONG IS IT?

"VIEWING PORN IS WRONG"

1 out of 2 adults

1 out of 3 teens and young adults

ON A LIST OF "BAD THINGS" A PERSON COULD DO, MOST PEOPLE RANK PORN PRETTY LOW

ADULTS 25+

Taking something that belongs to someone else	95%
Having a romantic relationship with someone other than a spouse	89%
Saying something that isn't true	87%
Overeating	58%
Wanting something that belongs to someone else	57%
Thinking negatively about someone with a different point of view	55%
Viewing pornographic images	54%
Reading erotic or pornographic content (no pictures)	46%
Not recycling	44%
Significant consumption of electricity or water	39%
Watching sexually explicit scenes on TV or in a movie	37%

TEENS AND YOUNG ADULTS RANK NOT RECYCLING AS MORE IMMORAL THAN VIEWING PORN

88% — Taking something that belongs to someone else

75% — Having a romantic relationship with someone other than a spouse

71% — Saying something that isn't true

56% — NOT RECYCLING

55% — Thinking negatively about someone with a different point of view

48% — Overeating

38% — Significant consumption of electricity or water

32% — Wanting something that belongs to someone else

32% — Viewing pornographic images

27% — Reading erotic or pornographic content (no pictures)

24% — Watching sexually explicit scenes on TV or in a movie

TEENS & YOUNG ADULTS

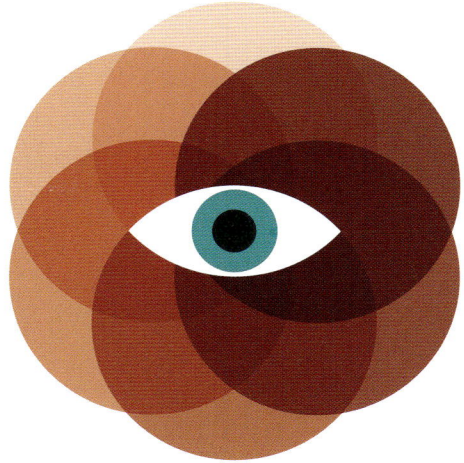

4.

THE IMPACT
OF PORN

While its social and economic significance are undeniable, pornography has thus far failed to attract a proportionate level of attention from scholars. For one thing, there is a general reluctance among funders to underwrite sexual research, but also logistical and ethical challenges in dealing with pornographic material and participants in the industry. Another challenge is finding control groups—especially males—who have not previously engaged with porn.[42]

Much of the existing research is conflicting and inconclusive when it comes to understanding the impact of pornography on individual mental and sexual health, interpersonal relationships and deviant behaviors. No clear consensus has yet emerged on a number of key issues.

> Most studies of pornography go no further than establishing correlations between how much people say they watch and their other characteristics. Various researchers have

found that reported porn use is higher among those with relationship difficulties, erectile dysfunction and many other social and medical problems. Heavy users are more likely to have become sexually active early, to regard sex as a mere physiological function, like eating or drinking, and to have tried to coerce others into sex. But no one knows which came first: the porn or the problem.[43]

We don't yet know the full impact of pornography on our lives.[44] Yet there does exist a body of research claiming that pornography has a significantly negative impact on society, relationships and individuals.

Let's take a brief tour of this research, alongside Barna's recent surveys of U.S. teens and adults. How do Americans' perceptions of porn's impact stack up against what science has to say?

SOCIETAL IMPACT

What kind of impact do you think widespread pornography use has on our society? Among U.S. adults 18 and older, 68 percent believe it has a negative impact on society and 10 percent believe its impact is positive. The rest are neutral on porn's societal impact (22%).

As we might expect, given their higher rates of porn use, Millennials are twice as likely as the norm to say porn has a positive impact on society (19%) and more likely to say it has neither a positive nor negative impact (31%). At the same time, as we will explore in a later section, Millennials are also more likely to express feelings of guilt about their porn use. This could indicate an internal conflict between their desire for and belief in sexual freedom and the negative effects of porn use they are beginning to see as they emerge into adulthood. (As we saw in a similar question, older Millennials are more likely than young adults 18 to 24 to say porn is very or somewhat bad for society.)

One of the meta-themes of self-fulfillment is the separation of sex from love: Sex is an expected feature of dating, not a union that expresses lasting love. At the same time, the influence of porn is increasing men's objectification of women. What will these two trends produce? How will they affect women? How will they affect men? What, if anything, can the Church do to help?

THE IMPACT OF PORN ON SOCIETY, BY GENERATION
% among U.S. adults 18 and older

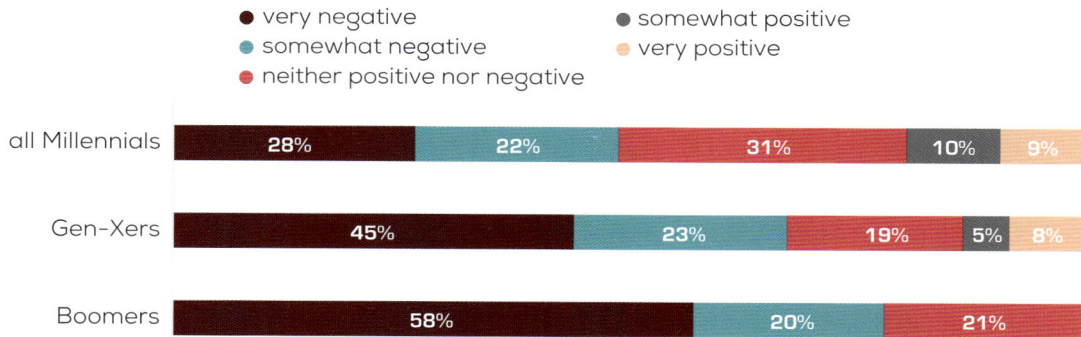

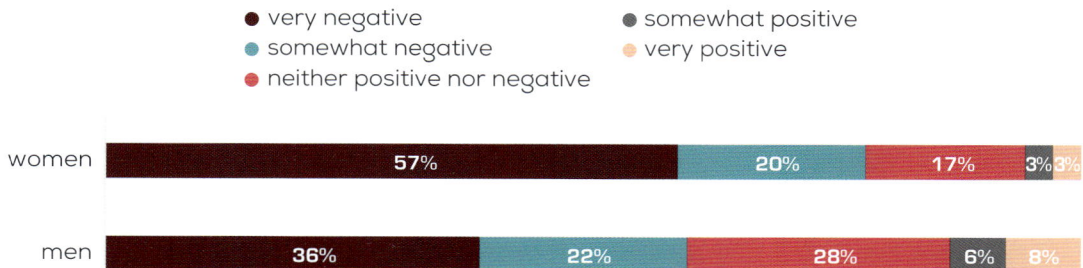

● very negative
● somewhat negative
● neither positive nor negative
● somewhat positive
● very positive

Generation	very negative	somewhat negative	neither positive nor negative	somewhat positive	very positive
all Millennials	28%	22%	31%	10%	9%
Gen-Xers	45%	23%	19%	5%	8%
Boomers	58%	20%	21%		

Gender Inequality and Misogyny

As we might expect, more women than men have negative views about porn's impact on society. Of course, far fewer women than men use porn, but it's unlikely this is the only factor in women's assessment of porn's effects. Many women are aware that porn is becoming ever more degrading and violent, and likely worry this trend will have negative consequences for their lives and relationships.

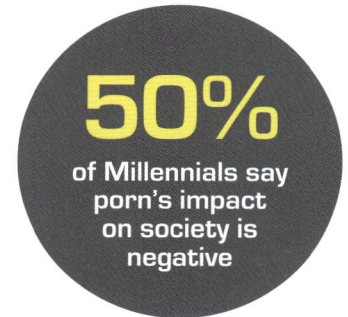

50% of Millennials say porn's impact on society is negative

THE IMPACT OF PORN ON SOCIETY, BY GENDER
% among U.S. adults 18 and older

● very negative
● somewhat negative
● neither positive nor negative
● somewhat positive
● very positive

Gender	very negative	somewhat negative	neither positive nor negative	somewhat positive	very positive
women	57%	20%	17%	3%	3%
men	36%	22%	28%	6%	8%

PORNOGRAPHY OBJECTIFIES AND DEMEANS WOMEN

Pornography, particularly in its more hardcore iterations, objectifies and demeans women. "By presenting women in terms of their sexuality, pornography of its very nature promotes a woman's physical form above all other characteristics as their defining feature."[45] Anti-pornography feminists such as Catherine MacKinnon and Robert Jensen have argued that, through pornography, women as a group are reduced to the status of mere tools for men's purposes—sexual objects available for their consumption.[46] This is, by definition, objectification.

This is by no means a problem isolated to porn: 83 percent of U.S. women and 80 percent of men agree with the statement "our culture objectifies women's bodies." But porn participates in and even exacerbates the cultural crisis.

Common tropes in pornography are sex stereotyped, wherein men are portrayed as violent, dominant, high-status professionals, while women are often low-status housewives who are nonviolent and submissive. In a 2014 study, consuming porn with these stereotypes was found to affect real-life attitudes. College-age men who consumed sexually explicit media with themes of male dominance expressed less progressive attitudes toward women.[47] Further, a UCLA study demonstrated that exposure to violent pornography hardens misogynistic attitudes.[48]

But much of porn today goes beyond "mere" objectification and misogyny. In a study of the top-50 rented porn films, physical aggression occurred in 88 percent of scenes, while verbal aggression was portrayed in 48 percent of scenes.[49] It's even worse in an amateur, hardcore style of pornography called "gonzo porn," in which violence and degradation are commonplace.

The story gonzo porn tells about women, according to Gail Dines, author of *Pornland*, is consistent: "Women are always ready for sex, and are enthusiastic to do whatever men want, irrespective of how painful, humiliating, or harmful."[50] Dines argues that sex in porn is designed to deliver the maximum amount of degradation, validating male dominance and female submission.

One study found that violent pornography increases the acceptance of rape myths.[51] *Rape myths* are erroneous ideas about rape; for example, victims of rape are partially to blame for the crime, rape is not a serious crime and rapists should not get tough sentences. Another study showed that heavy exposure to nonviolent pornography correlates with trivializing rape as a criminal offense.[52]

Exploitation

Although most adult film studios have improved their practices in terms of contracts, pay and working conditions, including the recent Los Angeles County measure that requires condom use in adult films, many actors—particularly those in gonzo and other amateur porn—tell stories of abuse and exploitation, particularly sexual and psychological abuse.[53]

There are also claims of a link between pornography and sex trafficking. According to Shared Hope International's report on the demand for sex trafficking, use of pornography is the primary gateway to the purchase of humans for sex.[54] The Freedom Youth Project reports that thousands of trafficked children and young adults have been forced to make pornographic films.[55] In their book *Renting Lacy*, the authors claim that many women and children who are sexually exploited and trafficked are also used for the production of pornography. Acts of prostitution are filmed and distributed without consent of the victims.[56]

Another devastating reality of the industry is child pornography. Over five million reports related to child sexual exploitation have been made to The National Center for Missing and Exploited Children's CyberTipline since it was created. In 2013 the organization reviewed 22 million images of suspected child sexual abuse in its victim identification program—a *5,000-percent* increase from 2007. One in five identified offenders had images of children younger than three years old, two in five younger than six years old, and eight in 10 younger than 12 years old.[57] And the use of child pornography continues to grow.

Human trafficking and the sexual exploitation of children are part of the porn world, and seem like natural places for Christians to push back pornography's reach. Who can your local congregation partner with to fight these tragedies in your community?

TEEN AND ADULTS
WHO SEEK OUT PORN
DAILY AND WEEKLY
ARE LESS LIKELY
THAN OTHERS TO
CATEGORIZE MORE
EXTREME FORMS
OF PORNOGRAPHY
AS WRONG

This may be due in part to a relaxation of moral standards that correlates to more frequent porn use. Teens and adults who seek out porn daily and weekly are less likely than others to categorize more extreme forms of pornography as wrong.

SEXUAL IMAGES THAT ARE WRONG, BY FREQUENCY OF USE

base: teens and adults 13 and older % "wrong"	% daily	% weekly	% once or twice a month	% less often
children under the age of 12	91	97	98	99
sexual acts that are not consensual	80	87	91	91
sexual acts that may be forced or painful	66	72	75	91
teens	54	71	82	84
someone depicted in a demeaning way	45	59	70	84

Only half of daily porn users say porn featuring teens is wrong

Racism

According to Gail Dines, "Blatant examples of racism that were once commonplace in mainstream media have become less acceptable. But this is not so for the porn industry, which gets away with a level of racism that is breathtaking in its contempt and loathing for people of color."[58] For example, there are overtly racist titles that feature black men and an entire porn genre called "interracial." Roles and scenarios often rely on offensive racial stereotypes, such as black men cast as drug dealers or criminals. White women often refuse to do scenes with black men, or ask for extra money to do so.[59]

Women of color are generally relegated to gonzo films, where past and present racial stereotypes (of Asians and

Latinas as well as African Americans) are side-by-side with demeaning gender tropes. This represents, Dines argues, a "dual subordination," debasing a performer as both a woman and as a person of color.[60] Adding injury to insult, black female actors also earn half to three-quarters what white women earn for the same work.[61]

PERSONAL IMPACT

Of the teens and adults who report seeking porn at least occasionally (51%), only 5 percent say porn has negatively affected their sex life or has hurt their relationships. On the other hand, 28 percent say porn has positively affected their sex life.

PERSONAL IMPACT OF PORN,
BY MARITAL STATUS AND GENERATION

base: adults 25+ who seek out porn at least occasionally	% married (25+)	% single (25+)	% Millennials	% Gen-Xers	% Boomers
It has positively affected your sex life	31	23	28	30	20
You feel a sense of guilt when you use porn	16	14	22	17	17
It sometimes hurts your relationships	6	2	6	5	2
It has negatively affected your sex life	5	4	6	3	8

Millennials are somewhat more likely than other age groups to say they feel a sense of guilt related to their porn use (22% compared to 17% among Gen-Xers and Boomers). They are also more likely to use porn and to use porn more often—so a greater proportion who reports feelings of guilt makes sense in that regard.

Among adults 25 and older, married (16%) and single (14%) adults are about equally likely to feel guilty about their porn use. Marrieds (31%), however, are more likely than singles (23%) to say porn has positively affected their sex life. It is conceivable that married adults who watch porn in isolation perceive a negative effect on their relationships while those who watch porn with their spouse view the effects as positive. This is supported by the fact that marrieds are less likely than singles to use porn for the purpose of personal arousal (see chapter 2).

Addiction and Neurological Conditioning

While pathological gambling and compulsive eating have received greater attention in functional and behavioral studies, evidence increasingly supports the description of compulsive sexual behaviors as addictions.[62] Studies have consistently found striking similarities between porn use and drug use when it comes to brain activity. A Cambridge University study found neural reactivity to sexually explicit cues were similar to the reactivity identified in drug studies. Porn addicts in the Cambridge study fit the addiction model of "wanting it more" but not "liking it more."[63]

A German study found that longer durations of porn consumption correlate with less reward circuit activation while viewing sexual photos, which suggests eventual desensitization.[64] Psychiatrist Norman Doidge, in his book *The Brain That Changes Itself,* presents evidence that the content viewers find exciting changes as websites introduce themes and scripts that alter viewers' brains without their awareness. Because neural plasticity is competitive, the brain maps for new, exciting images at the expense of what a person had previously found attractive.[65]

STUDIES HAVE CONSISTENTLY FOUND STRIKING SIMILARITIES BETWEEN PORN USE AND DRUG USE WHEN IT COMES TO BRAIN ACTIVITY

As with drug addiction, the urge to escalate is a real possibility. As some users become desensitized to "regular" porn through consistent consumption, they experience an increased appetite for more deviant and cruel images and scenarios.

The greatest concern about neurological effects center on teenagers, who are now likely to see a vast amount of pornography long before they become sexually active—and before their brains are finished developing. In 2013 the Office of the Children's Commissioner in England assessed the effects of porn and concluded that pornography appeared to have a negative impact on young people, in particular by creating unrealistic beliefs about sex. Meg Kaplan, a psychologist at Columbia University who treats those convicted of sex offenses, believes some sexual tastes are formed around the time of puberty, suggesting that ill-timed exposure to fetishistic or violent material could cause a lifelong predilection for that kind of sex.[66]

PORNOGRAPHY APPEARS TO HAVE A NEGATIVE IMPACT ON YOUNG PEOPLE, IN PARTICULAR BY CREATING UNREALISTIC BELIEFS ABOUT SEX

Erectile Dysfunction

A popular argument online and in the media claims that pornography use, particularly in excess, leads to erectile dysfunction (ED) even in young men. Various studies have reported up to 60 percent of subjects had difficulty achieving erections / arousal with real partners, yet could achieve erections using porn.[67] Further, a recent study in the *Journal of Sexual Medicine* suggests that an increase in erectile dysfunction in younger men may be related to porn use.[68] However, there are two other recent studies that show no link between porn and ED—so the jury is still out on this claim.[69]

RELATIONAL IMPACT

What is the purpose of sex? The traditional Christian view is that sex unites a woman and a man in marriage. This view is not generally accepted by the broader culture, however. The greatest cultural consensus has coalesced around "to express intimacy between two people who love each other," but even this understanding of sex is less common among younger generations. Conversely, the idea that sex is for self-expression and personal fulfillment is more popular among young adults than older Americans.

THE PURPOSE OF SEX, BY GENERATION

base: U.S. adults 18 and older (multiple response)	% all Millennials	% Gen-Xers	% Boomers
To express intimacy between two people who love each other	56	57	73
To reproduce / to have children	51	52	71
To connect with another person in an enjoyable way	49	44	44
For self-expression and personal fulfillment	41	31	33
To satisfy a biological need, not including reproduction	37	33	44
To unite a man and woman in marriage	32	35	50

These trends may or may not be *caused* by porn use, but certainly porn's ubiquity among younger Americans is in the mix of factors that inform their views. It's not hard to see how the morality of self-fulfillment—expressed here in the view that sex is for self-expression and personal fulfillment—can justify not only porn use but also other sexual activities divorced from relational intimacy and commitment.

Changing perceptions about the purpose of sex likely influence the amount of porn people consume. But just as likely is that the increasing amount of porn people consume contributes to a more carnal, less relational, view of sex. These factors may form an iterative cycle.

Unfortunately, porn's relational impact likely goes beyond shaping people's perceptions of sex. One study looked at the effect on male and female participants of consuming nonviolent pornographic material and found that participants reported less satisfaction with their intimate partner, specifically with their partner's affection, physical appearance, sexual curiosity and sexual performance.[70]

In his essay "Pornography's Effects on Adults and Children," Dr. Victor Cline argues that adults who regularly masturbate to pornography risk disturbing the bonded relationship with their spouse or partner. Doing so, he writes,

> dramatically reduces their capacity to love (e.g., it results in a marked dissociation of sex from friendship, affection, caring, and other normal healthy emotions and traits which help marital relationships). In time, the "high" obtained from masturbating to pornography becomes more important than real life relationships.[71]

Similarly, Pamela Paul, author of *Pornified*, found that some casual users of pornography have trouble achieving orgasm with their partner unless they are actively thinking about pornography.[72]

Another study found consumption of Internet porn was positively associated with having multiple sexual partners and engaging in both paid sex and extramarital sex.[73] In another, researchers Zillman and Bryant claim that pornography use creates doubts about the value of marriage, decreases the desire to have children and causes users to view non-monogamous relationships as normal and natural.[74] Another study suggests that Internet porn use can undermine

THE MORALITY OF SELF-FULLFILLMENT CAN JUSTIFY NOT ONLY PORN USE BUT ALSO OTHER SEXUAL ACTIVITIES DIVORCED FROM RELATIONAL INTIMACY AND COMMITMENT

marital exclusivity and fidelity. "Partners feel betrayed when they discover that their partner has been viewing pornography, which is perceived as infidelity."[75] Women reported a decrease in sexual intimacy and closeness due to their partner's porn use and "described their partner's sexual advances as conveying a message of objectification as opposed to meaningful interaction."[76] There are also claims that pornography has contributed to an increase in sexless marriages.[77]

Pornified Sex

Cindy Gallop, creator of MakeLoveNotPorn.com remarked in her TED Talk—which, to date, has been viewed nearly 5 million times on YouTube—"Guys watch porn and when they go to bed with a real woman, all they think about is recreating that scenario."[78] Empirical and anecdotal evidence seem to agree with her. Researchers at London University published a study examining whether porn played a part in young people's decisions to engage in anal sex. "Many of the young men described pressing girlfriends to consent; young women said they continued to be asked, sometimes forcefully, even after repeated refusals."[79] *GQ* published an op-ed from a sexually active young woman protesting the increasing numbers of men who expect pornified sex and seem to believe all women enjoy demeaning "dirty talk."[80]

And these effects may be trickling down. Psychologist Catherine Steiner-Adair interviewed 1,000 children ages 4 to 18 across the United States for her book *The Big Disconnect*. She found a marked tendency among even young boys to approach girls they like in a sexually aggressive manner.[81]

Sexual Violence

As we've noted, pornography has become increasingly violent in recent decades. But is there a relationship between violent porn and actual sexual violence? Again, the research shows mixed results.

According to Cindy Gallop, men watch porn and then think about what they've watched when they interact sexually with their wives. One partner comes to sex looking for self-fulfillment while the other hopes for intimate connection. It's hard to see how a marriage can survive under these circumstances, even if the husband is no longer actively using porn. How can we help couples heal as individuals and heal their relationship? Is it even possible?

In one study, men with higher past exposure to violent pornography were six times more likely to report having raped someone compared to those who reported low exposure.[82] Another showed correlations between use of all types of pornography (softcore, hardcore, violent and rape) and the likelihood of sexual coercion.[83]

Mary Anne Layden, PhD, is a psychotherapist and Director of the Sexual Trauma and Psychopathology Program at the University of Pennsylvania's Center for Cognitive Therapy. She has testified before the U.S. Congress on multiple occasions. In a 2011 briefing for the Kansas legislature on the connection of pornography to crime, she reported that she had been doing work for more than 10 years before realizing she had not treated a single case of sexual violence that did not include pornography. Dr. Layden found that the earlier young males are exposed to pornography, the more likely they are to engage in non-consensual sex, and that the more pornography females use, the more likely they are to be victims of non-consensual sex. "Pornography," she says, "is an equal opportunity toxin for both males and females."

In her book *Dangerous Relationships: Pornography, Misogyny and Rape*, Diana Russell offers evidence that pornography is a causal factor for rape because it has been shown to predispose some men to desire rape or intensify this desire, to undermine some men's internal or social inhibitions against acting out rape desires, and to weaken some potential victims' ability to avoid or resist rape.[84]

On the other hand, another study assessed the impact of anti-pornography statutes in four U.S. states on sex crimes. The number of arrests for rape, prostitution and other sex offenses reflected no significant change before and after the statutes went into effect.[85] If porn inevitably leads to sexual violence, one might expect the number of arrests to fall if access to porn is limited.

One researcher reviewed a number of studies on the links between exposure to sexually explicit material and sexual violence and found conflicting results. These correlative inconsistencies might be chalked up to different methodologies, measures and

IS THERE A RELATIONSHIP BETWEEN VIOLENT PORN AND ACTUAL SEXUAL VIOLENCE?

genres of porn included in the studies—it's all but impossible to say for sure.[86]

According to journalist and anti-porn activist Robert Jensen, if the question is whether pornography *causes* rape, the answer is almost always going to be no. He argues, "Since some men who use pornography don't rape, and some men who rape don't use pornography, pornography is neither a necessary nor sufficient condition for rape."[87] But if we go beyond a simple cause-and-effect model, Jensen continues, the better question would be, *Is pornography ever a factor that contributes to rape?* Few critics of porn contend that it is ever the sole, direct *cause* of sexual violence, but Jensen believes the discussion ought to center around whether porn is *implicated* in sexual violence.[88]

CHURCH IMPACT

PORN *IS* A PROBLEM FOR THE CHURCH, BUT PRACTICING CHRISTIANS ARE A FLOODBANK AGAINST THE CASCADING IMPACTS OF PORN ON PEOPLE, RELATIONSHIPS AND SOCIETY

Large majorities of practicing Christians (75%), senior pastors (92%) and youth pastors (94%) believe that porn is a bigger problem for the Church now than it was 20 years ago.

When pastors consider their own congregations, however, just two out of five say porn use is a major (3%) or significant (35%) problem. Half say it is only a minor problem (50%), and the remaining pastors believe it's not really an issue for their church. Interestingly, in a study among church leaders on discipleship, the vast majority of pastors said the Church as a whole is doing a poor job of discipleship—but their own congregation is pretty effective.[89] There could be a tendency among pastors to be pessimistic about the broader Church and optimistic about their local community of faith.

According to these same leaders, married men are the group most likely to ask the pastor for help dealing with their porn use. As the following comparison chart shows, among practicing Christians single men and teenage boys seek out porn more often than married men—but they may not experience the negative relational effects that could prompt married men to ask for help.

Compared to the proportion of practicing Christian women and teen girls who seek porn at least occasionally, few ask for help from their pastor for dealing with their porn use. This reticence may be due in part to the social stigma associated with female porn use or to the fact that most pastors are men, which adds a layer of social and sexual complexity to the pastor-parishioner relationship.

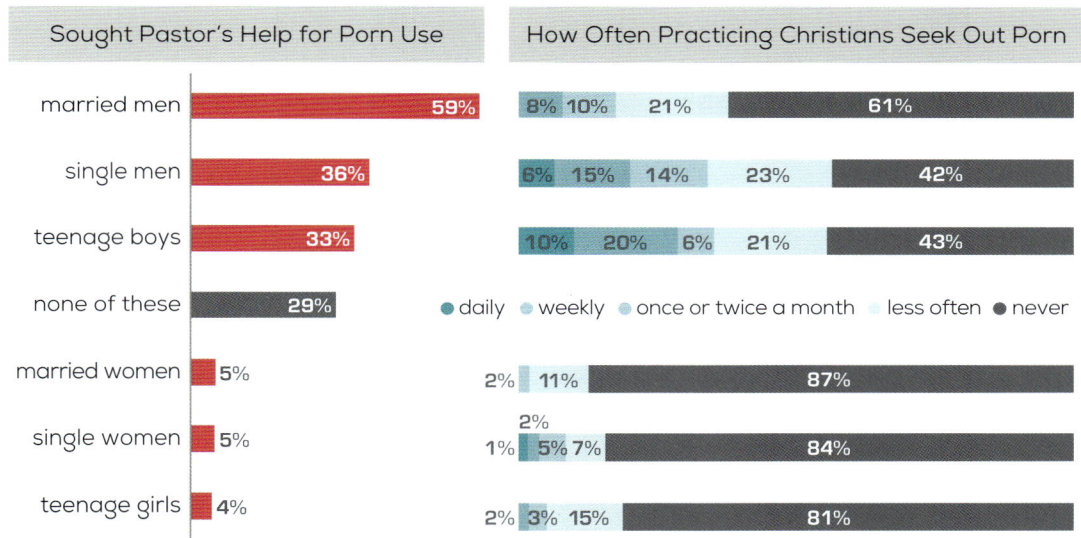

Sought Pastor's Help for Porn Use

married men	59%
single men	36%
teenage boys	33%
none of these	29%
married women	5%
single women	5%
teenage girls	4%

How Often Practicing Christians Seek Out Porn

	daily	weekly	once or twice a month	less often	never
married men	8%	10%	21%		61%
single men	6%	15%	14%	23%	42%
teenage boys	10%	20%	6%	21%	43%
married women		2%	11%		87%
single women	1%	2% 5%	7%		84%
teenage girls	2%	3%	15%		81%

Whether porn is a bigger problem for the Church now than in the past, it's clear that a practicing Christian faith has a profound influence on a person's porn habits. Among every age group and gender, practicing Christians seek porn less often than those who do not practice Christianity. (To see side-by-side comparisons, check out the infographic "Who Looks and How Often?" on page 32.)

This is good news. Porn *is* a problem for the Church—a problem that must not be ignored—but practicing Christians are a floodbank against the cascading impacts of porn on people, relationships and society.

▶ Q&A WITH THE NATIONAL CENTER ON SEXUAL EXPLOITATION

THE NATIONAL CENTER ON SEXUAL EXPLOITATION

NCOSE is the leading national organization addressing the public health crisis of pornography and exposing the links between all forms of sexual exploitation. NCOSE embraces a mission to defend human dignity and to advocate for the universal right to sexual justice, which is freedom from sexual exploitation, objectification and violence. To this end, NCOSE operates on the cutting edge of policy activism to combat corporate and government policies that foster sexual exploitation, to advance public education and empowerment, and foster united action through the international Coalition to End Sexual Exploitation.

www.EndSexualExploitation.org

Q: You've done a lot of work with women who were formerly in the porn industry. Do you have a story you could share about their experiences? What would you want people who are regularly watching porn to know about those who work in the industry?

A: All human beings have an *inherent* dignity that must be respected and defended. Pornography is an attack on the dignity of those who are used to make it.

"Victoria" (name changed to protect her identity) was one of the first pornography performers that connected with The National Center on Sexual Exploitation. Dawn Hawkins, NCOSE's Executive Director, had the opportunity to meet and talk with Victoria about her first time participating in a pornography shoot.

Victoria ran away from a difficult home situation after being raped when she was 16 years old, and found herself alone and on the streets. She was quickly recruited to "work" in a strip club. She felt like it was her only option for survival.

She hated the experience and the constant fear she lived in. When an "agent" showed up at the club and told Victoria she could make more money working only one or two days a month in a totally safe environment, doing only things she felt comfortable doing, while being treated like a star, she thought it sounded like a great opportunity.

Nevertheless, Victoria was hesitant and scared of what would be expected of her. So the agent helped her make a list of the types of acts that she was not comfortable doing, explaining that she would never have to do those things. At the top of her list, Victoria wrote that she did not want to have sex with more than one man at a time.

When she showed up for her first shoot, Victoria found herself in the exact situation she had explained she did not want to do. The scene was a "gangbang." When she objected, her agent said that she had signed a contract and that legal action would be taken against her if she did not proceed. Victoria was the only woman on the entire set that day and felt completely powerless to say no. And so the shoot proceeded.

It was like reliving her earlier experience of rape all over again. After the filming, she felt completely broken. She had no more confidence or power at all. All she had left was the money she had been given—more than she had ever received before. When they called again urging her to do another shoot, she felt like nothing mattered anymore, and so went on to make many more films.

Dawn has heard dozens of stories similar to this one. Performers, both those currently performing and those who have left the industry, have shared with her about numerous experiences of being forced, coerced and manipulated into participating in sex acts they were not comfortable doing or never consented to do. The pornography industry is in the business of pushing boundaries; it doesn't matter if the women are yelling *no* or *stop*.

We especially want people who watch pornography to know that the images they are watching are, very often, acts of real abuse against real women. From the viewers' side of the screen, there is no way to know if women are "consenting" and "acting" or being forced. We want people to know that pornography preys on those who are vulnerable to exploitation due to their immaturity (i.e., "barely legal" age) or desperate financial circumstances, and that many performers are manipulated and coerced by boyfriends, husbands, parents and so-called managers. We want people to know that many women in pornography come from broken backgrounds and their tragic experiences have been used against them, conditioning them to accept abuse for the entertainment and enjoyment of the viewer.

When people become educated about the multifaceted harms of pornography and about how their own pornography use is a form of participation in sexual exploitation, some start to care. The abuse and degradation inherent in all pornography, when addressed in the light of day, ignites a sense of compassion and urgency in people who do not want to stand by while others suffer.

NCOSE's work to educate the public has led to increased awareness about pornography as a *public health crisis*. The state of Utah is considering a resolution that would officially declare pornography a public health hazard, and other states may follow their lead. More individuals and experts than ever are rising up to speak out about pornography's harms.

NCOSE also leads an international coalition of organizations and advocates that helps to educate leaders in various disciplines about the links between all forms of sexual exploitation. Citizen activists are also on the rise, addressing the presence of pornography in libraries and schools or working to hold corporations accountable for policies that facilitate sexual exploitation. When an individual becomes educated, another advocate joins the movement.

▶ Q&A WITH ROBERT JENSEN

ROBERT JENSEN
Professor of journalism and outspoken critic of pornography

Robert is a professor in the School of Journalism at the University of Texas at Austin and a board member of the Third Coast Activist Resource Center in Austin. He is the author of *Plain Radical: Living, Loving, and Learning to Leave the Planet Gracefully*. Jensen's other books include *Arguing for Our Lives: A User's Guide to Constructive Dialogue*; *All My Bones Shake: Seeking a Progressive Path to the Prophetic Voice*; *Getting Off: Pornography and the End of Masculinity*; *The Heart of Whiteness: Confronting Race, Racism and White Privilege*; *Citizens of the Empire: The Struggle to Claim Our Humanity*; and *Writing Dissent: Taking Radical Ideas from the Margins to the Mainstream*.

www.RobertWJensen.org
@jensenrobertw

Q: Since your book *Getting Off: Pornography and the End of Masculinity* was first published in 2007, the trends you documented of increasing cruelty toward and degradation of women have continued unabated in porn. Yet there seems to be a discrepancy between the soaring popularity of this kind of explicit content and people's views of it. Barna found that seven in 10 Americans 13 and older consider depicting someone in porn "in a demeaning way" is wrong; eight in 10 say porn with "sexual acts that may be forced or painful" is wrong; and nine in 10 say "sexual acts that are not consensual" portrayed in porn are wrong. What, if anything, can you make of this disconnect?

A: The results may mean that many of the people who use sexually explicit material that is openly misogynistic recognize that such images violate their own moral principles of respect, dignity and equality. These people might not endorse a feminist critique of that misogyny, or even know that such a critique exists, but they intuitively understand the power of that critical perspective.

Q: You have written about the "cruel boredom" of pornography, which continually ups the ante on brutality and humiliation to provoke an emotional response from male viewers and keep them coming back for more. Barna found that, among teens ages 13 to 17 (46%) and young adults ages 18 to 24 (42%), "boredom" is the second most common reason for seeking porn, behind "personal arousal" (the top reason among every age group). Thinking about your scholarly work in this area, how likely is it that the boredom expressed by younger porn users could up the ante even further? Why?

A: If the joy and passion of sex is about human connection, then it's clear why pornography will always be "boring," in the sense that it turns a complex human practice into something dull and repetitive. That's why the images continue to get more cruel and degrading to women, and also more openly racist—pornographers need to counter the banality of sexually explicit material. But boredom in this case perhaps reflects a larger way in which the hyper-mediated experience of young people—not just pornography, but video games, movies, television and other kinds of screens—fails to satisfy our needs for meaningful connection. The lives of many people are saturated with various kinds of stimulation that don't meet deeper human needs, and in the end that likely is experienced as boredom.

Q: Another major theme in your work is the "end of masculinity," by which you mean the end of our culture's acceptance and even promotion of male dominance and aggression. According to Barna's survey, 16 percent of U.S. women and teen girls report actively seeking porn at least once per month. Do you think women using porn could be a hopeful sign for the end of masculinity—and if so, in what ways? Or if not, what do you see at work in the growing trend of women's porn use?

A: I would like to see us abandon our celebration of masculinity and ask how male humans can stop worrying about "how to be man" and concentrate on simply being human. My critique of pornography is part of a larger feminist project of challenging male dominance throughout society, which requires us to critique masculinity. Unfortunately, increased pornography use by women doesn't further that goal. If the pornography that women use simply replicates the male-supremacist values of most sexually explicit material, then nothing is gained. If alternative forms of sexually explicit material avoid the misogyny, that's an improvement, but it still leaves people seeking intimate human experience through a screen, and there's no reason to think that is helping us create a more humane and flourishing culture.

SPECIAL REPORT
COVENANT EYES

Internet filtering *with accountability* is more effective than filtering alone.

Covenant Eyes, a service that offers "Internet accountability," partnered with Josh McDowell Ministry to sponsor *The Porn Phenomenon* research. Covenant Eyes offers content blocking and filtering, like many similar services, but also integrates accountability into its service. The software monitors Internet devices for websites visited, search terms used and videos watched, and collects all the data in a report that is shared with a person or people designated by the Covenant Eyes user—people who can then hold the user accountable for his or her Internet habits.

As one aspect of *The Porn Phenomenon* study, Barna researchers surveyed Covenant Eyes members to identify how their perceptions and habits differ, if at all, from the general U.S. population.

First, Barna found that Covenant Eyes members are much more likely than their age counterparts in the general population to view porn negatively. For example, teens and young adults who use Covenant Eyes are about four times more likely than other Americans 24 and younger to say porn is very bad for society (85% vs. ~20%). Likewise, Covenant Eyes teens and young adults are far more likely to say that, if and when they talk with their friends about porn, the tone of the conversation is negative: 73 percent say the way they talk about it is "disagreeable," compared to only 11 percent of other teens and 5 percent of other young adults. Also similarly, greater majorities of Covenant Eyes users say porn that features children under the age of 12, non-consensual sex acts, sex that is forced or painful, demeaning depictions of people, teens, sex between two people of the same gender and sex between more than two people at once are "always wrong."

Second, because there is some skepticism among ministry leaders about the effectiveness of Internet filtering software as a tool for avoiding porn use—just 30 percent of senior pastors and 25 percent of youth pastors say it is very effective—researchers compared frequency of use between Covenant Eyes users and those in the general population w*ho have installed porn-blocking Internet filters*. The data shows that Internet filtering *with accountability*— the service offered by Covenant Eyes—is more effective at curbing porn use than porn-blocking filters alone.

HOW FREQUENTLY PEOPLE SEEK OUT PORN, BY INTERNET FILTERING SERVICE

% among U.S. adults 25+ and Covenant Eyes members

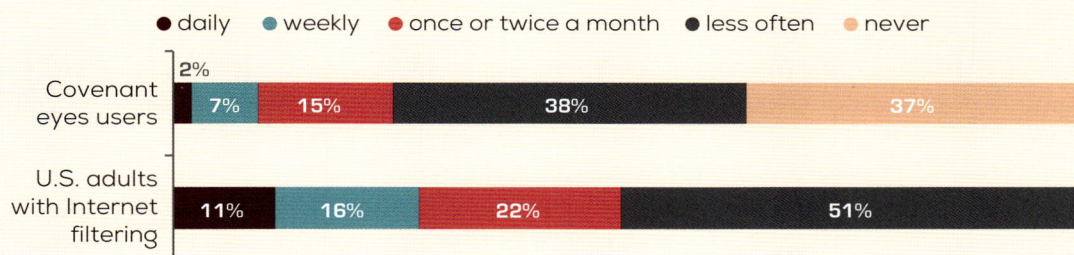

● daily ● weekly ● once or twice a month ● less often ● never

Covenant eyes users: 2% | 7% | 15% | 38% | 37%

U.S. adults with Internet filtering: 11% | 16% | 22% | 51%

This finding is not surprising when we consider how highly accountability groups are rated by ministry leaders as effective solutions for people who want to stop using porn. (Fifty-two percent of senior pastors and 72 percent of youth pastors have recommended accountability to those who have sought their help.)

It is difficult to say why no respondents who have installed blocking filters have been able to stop searching for porn. In some cases those who install content-blocking filters alone may actually be *more* tempted to view porn than they would be without filters, because getting around the filter is an attractive challenge. Regardless, it's clear that an accountability relationship is far more effective for those who want to limit or stop their searches for porn.

MOST PORN USERS ARE OK WITH HOW MUCH PORN THEY USE—BUT PRACTICING CHRISTIANS ARE DIVIDED

% among all adults and teens 13 and older who actively seek out porn at least occasionally

● All ● Practicing Christians

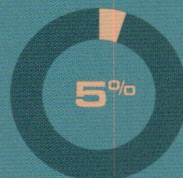

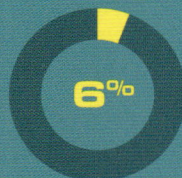

68% **39%** **14%** **21%** **18%** **40%**

I am comfortable with how much porn I use

I would rather not use it as much as I do, but some is OK

I would rather not use porn at all

54% OF PORN USERS SAY IT DOESN'T REALLY BOTHER THEM TO USE PORN

"I FEEL A SENSE OF GUILT WHEN I USE PORN"

1/5 of all porn users

1/3 of Practicing Christian porn users

MORE PEOPLE SAY PORN HAS POSITIVELY AFFECTED THEIR SEX LIFE THAN NEGATIVELY

● All
● Practicing Christians

5% **6%**

It has negatively affected my sex life

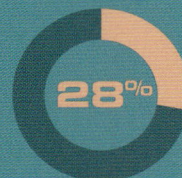

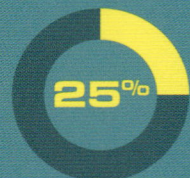

28% **25%**

It has positively affected my sex life

TRYING TO STOP?

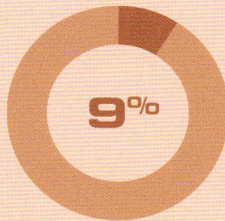 All  Practicing Christians

You have tried to stop using it, but have been unable to (or started again)

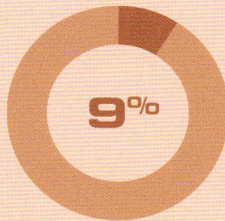
9%

16%

You are currently trying to stop using porn

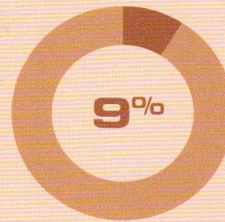
9%

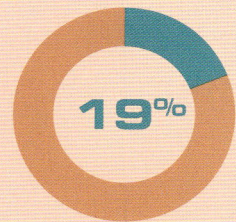
19%

Even for those who want to stop—most porn users do not have someone in their life who is helping them avoid pornography.

DO YOU HAVE ANYONE IN YOUR LIFE WHO IS HELPING YOU AVOID PORNOGRAPHY?

% among those who want to stop using pornography

- Yes
- No
- Not sure

Teens & Young adults
79%
21%

Adults 25+
87%
13%

IS THERE ANYONE WHO YOU THINK COULD HELP?

% among those who say no one is helping them avoid it now

Teens & Young adults
47%
33%
20%

Adults 25+
46%
38%
16%

WHO?
TEENS & YOUNG ADULTS: A FRIEND
ADULTS: MY SIGNIFICANT OTHER

WHAT IS THE BEST RESOURCE FOR DEALING WITH PORN USE?
CHRISTIAN ADULTS: PERSONAL COUNSELING
SENIOR PASTORS: MENTORING

Despite 70% of senior pastors saying porn is a "much bigger" problem for the Church now compared with 20 years ago, only 7 percent of pastors say their church has a ministry program for those struggling with porn.

5.

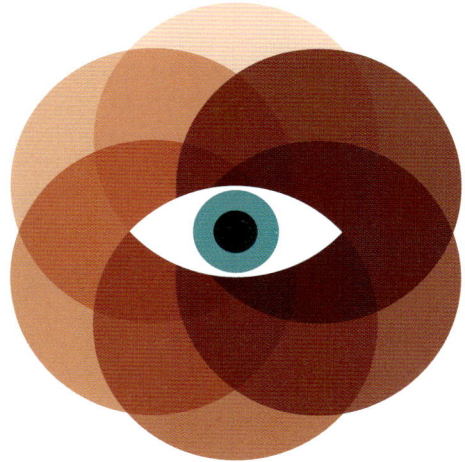

WHAT CAN WE DO ABOUT PORN?

Many leaders are aware that porn use is a problem for people and, thus, a problem for the Church. And so churches and parachurch men's ministries take a variety of approaches to meeting the challenge of pornography. Which approaches seem to be most effective? Is there something more or different that can be done?

Barna researchers identified some trends and opportunities.

WHAT WE *ARE* DOING

Among U.S. adults 25 and older, self-identified Christians find personal counseling and having a mentor to be the two most effective strategies for dealing with porn. It's not surprising that many people prefer avenues with greater levels of confidentiality. For Christians in particular, using porn comes with feelings of guilt and shame, and many local faith communities do not seem like safe places to admit a struggle with sexual sin. (This may be why pastors or spiritual advisors are low on the list of people who are helping those who want to stop using porn.)

DO YOU HAVE ANYONE IN YOUR LIFE WHO IS HELPING YOU AVOID PORNOGRAPHY?

% among U.S. teens, young adults and adults 25+ who would like to stop using porn

Teens & Young Adults

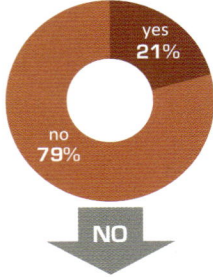

yes 21%
no 79%

Adults

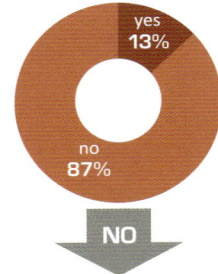

yes 13%
no 87%

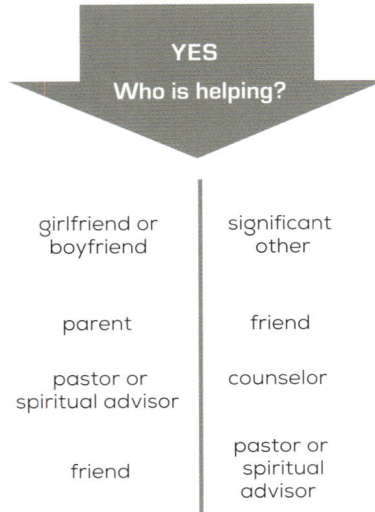

YES
Who is helping?

girlfriend or boyfriend	significant other
parent	friend
pastor or spiritual advisor	counselor
friend	pastor or spiritual advisor

NO

Anyone who could help?

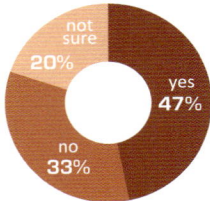

not sure 20%
yes 47%
no 33%

Top Person:
FRIEND

NO

Anyone who could help?

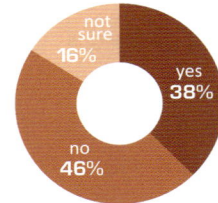

not sure 16%
yes 38%
no 46%

Top Person:
SIGNIFICANT OTHER

21%
of teens and young adults have someone to help them avoid porn

Yet the one-on-one element shared by counseling and mentoring offers more than confidentiality. It also holds out the promise of a deeper relational component that, for many people, is a necessary factor for their healing (since porn use is often a symptom of deeper relational pain).

It is, perhaps, understandable why Christian adults are not as excited about accountability groups: Sharing one's sexual sin with a wider circle of people sounds like a daunting prospect to many. Yet senior pastors seem to believe these groups can be as effective as one-on-one mentoring. Being in a group that openly talks about sexual struggles requires admission of one's guilt, the first step toward repentance. And the mutual vulnerability confession requires creates the kind of community that can support one another's recovery.

MOST EFFECTIVE RESOURCES FOR DEALING WITH PORN USE: CHRISTIAN ADULTS

% among U.S. self-identified Christians 25 and older

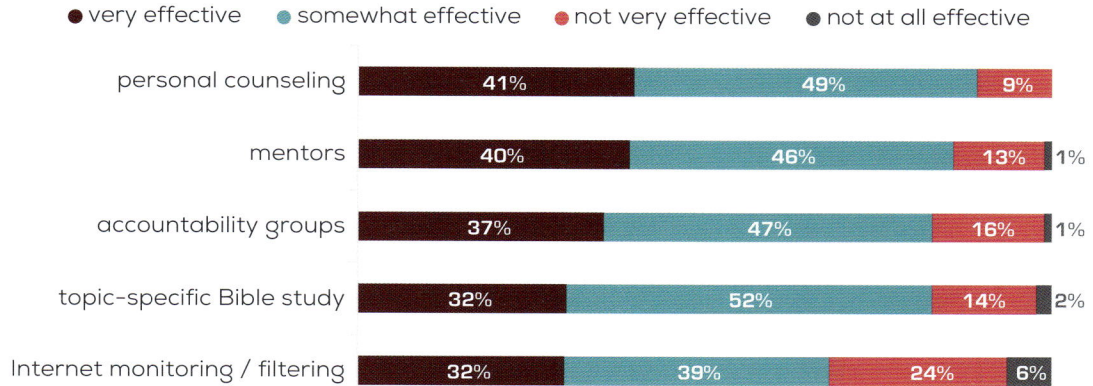

● very effective ● somewhat effective ● not very effective ● not at all effective

Resource	very effective	somewhat effective	not very effective	not at all effective
personal counseling	41%	49%	9%	
mentors	40%	46%	13%	1%
accountability groups	37%	47%	16%	1%
topic-specific Bible study	32%	52%	14%	2%
Internet monitoring / filtering	32%	39%	24%	6%

MOST EFFECTIVE RESOURCES FOR DEALING WITH PORN USE: SENIOR PASTORS

% among U.S. senior pastors

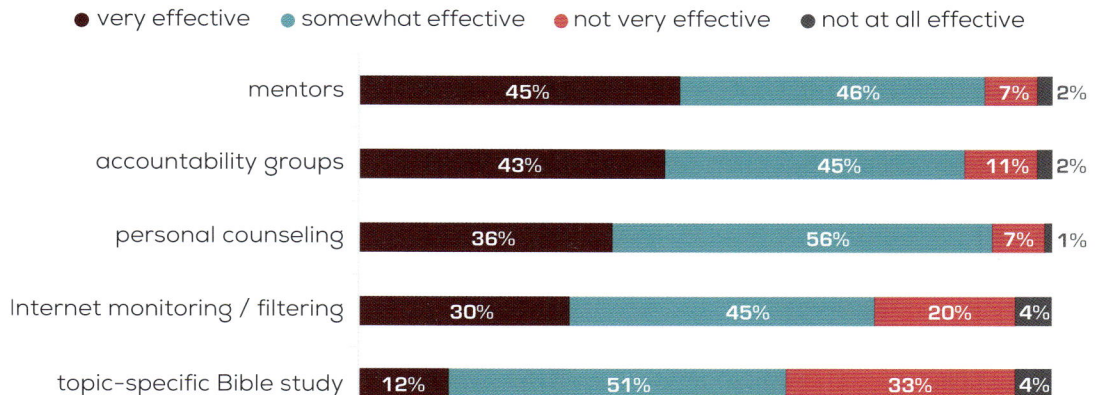

● very effective ● somewhat effective ● not very effective ● not at all effective

Resource	very effective	somewhat effective	not very effective	not at all effective
mentors	45%	46%	7%	2%
accountability groups	43%	45%	11%	2%
personal counseling	36%	56%	7%	1%
Internet monitoring / filtering	30%	45%	20%	4%
topic-specific Bible study	12%	51%	33%	4%

Both pastors and Christian adults are skeptical about the effectiveness of Internet monitoring or filtering software. Certainly this kind of intervention should not be a long-term standalone solution, since it doesn't address the whys behind a person's use of porn. But it *can* be helpful in the short term, both for the feeling of immediacy ("I need to do something about this *right now!*") and for interrupting habitual use. For long-term recovery, however, the relational component seems to be key.

While senior pastors say that mentors are the most effective way to address struggles with porn, fewer pastors recommend them as resources than recommend personal counseling, accountability groups or even Internet monitoring / filtering systems. (Software solutions likely rank so highly among pastors' recommendations because they are easy and immediate.) Mentors may not often be recommended because there simply aren't enough available.

Three-quarters of senior pastors feel well equipped to help those who struggle with porn (15% very, 58% somewhat)—but

Currently, many pastors do not look to mentors to help people overcome porn use—despite the fact that these relationships are effective. What methods can we use to identify, train and deploy more mentors?

TOP RESOURCES RECOMMENDED BY SENIOR PASTORS

% U.S. senior pastors

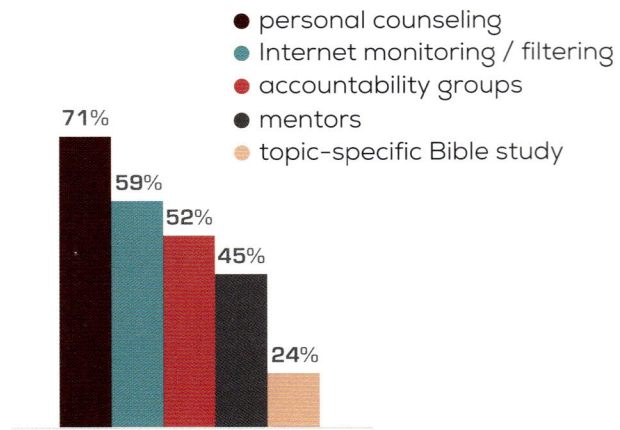

- ● personal counseling
- ● Internet monitoring / filtering
- ● accountability groups
- ● mentors
- ● topic-specific Bible study

71%
59%
52%
45%
24%

Christian adults are skeptical about their leaders' abilities in this area. Only 45 percent of self-identified Christians 25 and older say yes, their leaders are well equipped to help. About one in six say no (17%) and 38 percent are not sure.

Part of the uncertainty may have to do with the fact that only 7 percent of pastors report their church has a ministry program for those struggling with porn. (Among the churches that do have a program, the most common types are group counseling, small group Bible studies, individual counseling and making books and other content available.)

What We Are Doing for Youth

Youth ministry is ground zero for the porn phenomenon. Teens and young adults, as we've seen, are much more likely than older adults to use mobile technologies to view, receive, share and create sexually explicit content.

Barna asked adults 25 and older when they started viewing porn and found the likelihood of starting porn use before puberty doubles in each successively younger age cohort. That is, Gen-Xers (13%) are twice as likely as Boomers (6%) to say they began viewing porn before puberty, and older Millennials (27%) are twice as likely as Gen-Xers to say so.

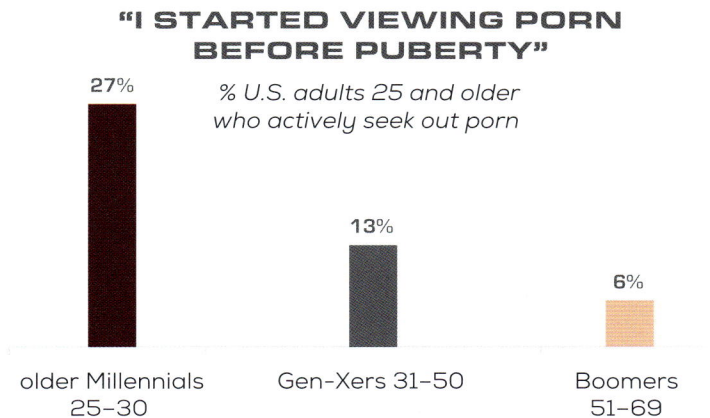

ONLY 7 PERCENT OF PASTORS SAY THEIR CHURCH HAS A MINISTRY PROGRAM FOR THOSE STRUGGLING WITH PORN

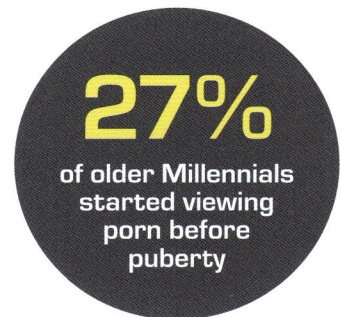

27%
of older Millennials started viewing porn before puberty

"I STARTED VIEWING PORN BEFORE PUBERTY"

% U.S. adults 25 and older who actively seek out porn

older Millennials 25–30	Gen-Xers 31–50	Boomers 51–69
27%	13%	6%

YOUTH MINISTRY IS GROUND ZERO FOR THE PORN PHENOMENON

It's a good bet this is true for even more young adults and teens.

Youth pastors seem to be aware of the urgency. More than nine out of 10 say porn is a major (55%) or significant (40%) problem for teens overall, and two-thirds say it is a major (14%) or significant (53%) problem specifically for the youth in their church.

HOW BIG OF A PROBLEM IS PORN AMONG TEENS?: YOUTH PASTORS

% among U.S. youth pastors

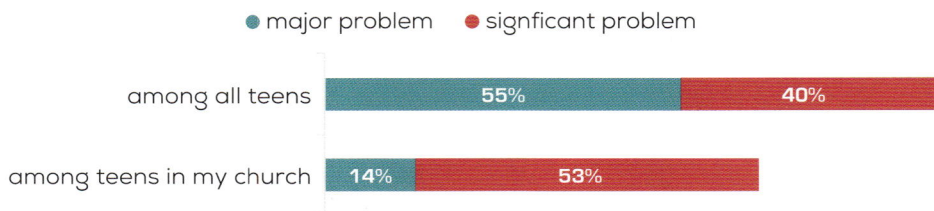

● major problem ● signficant problem

	major problem	signficant problem
among all teens	55%	40%
among teens in my church	14%	53%

Many believe porn is not the *most* urgent issue, however. Eight out of 10 say that spiritual immaturity among youth in their church is a bigger problem (79%); seven out of 10 that a lack of biblical knowledge is more pressing (71%); six out of 10 that self-indulgence (63%) or pride (59%) are bigger problems; and half that a lack of involvement in the church (50%) is a bigger issue.

So what are youth leaders doing to address the challenge of porn use among teens?

Youth pastors seem to be somewhat more consistent than senior pastors in recommending resources they believe will actually be effective. They are also inclined, however, to recommend Internet monitoring software even though they are skeptical about its effectiveness—probably for the same reasons explored above. When a teen comes to a youth leader asking for help to stop using porn, installing filtering software is a bandage that can be applied immediately.

MOST EFFECTIVE RESOURCES FOR DEALING WITH TEENS' PORN USE: YOUTH PASTORS

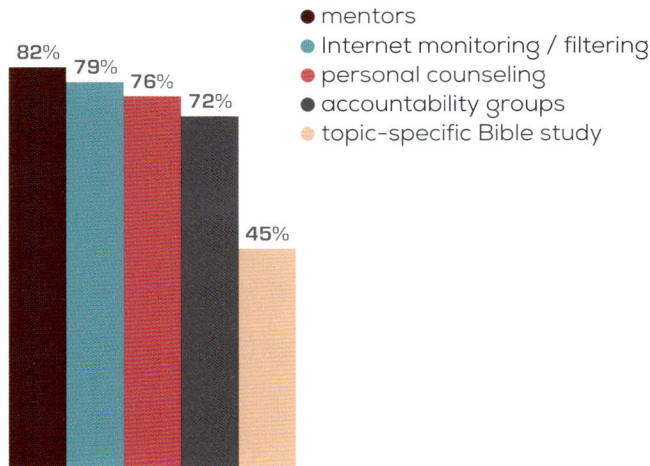

% among U.S. youth pastors

● very effective   ● somewhat effective   ● not very effective   ● not at all effective

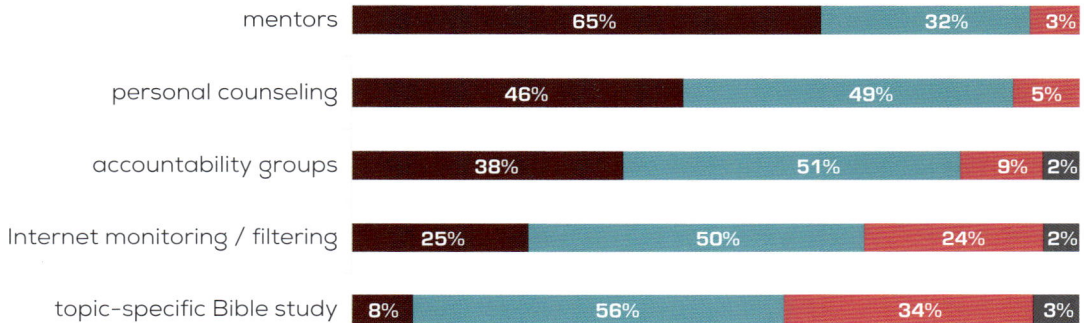

	very effective	somewhat effective	not very effective	not at all effective
mentors	65%	32%	3%	
personal counseling	46%	49%	5%	
accountability groups	38%	51%	9%	2%
Internet monitoring / filtering	25%	50%	24%	2%
topic-specific Bible study	8%	56%	34%	3%

TOP RESOURCES RECOMMENDED BY YOUTH PASTORS

% U.S. youth pastors

● mentors
● Internet monitoring / filtering
● personal counseling
● accountability groups
● topic-specific Bible study

- mentors: 82%
- Internet monitoring / filtering: 79%
- personal counseling: 76%
- accountability groups: 72%
- topic-specific Bible study: 45%

70% of self-identified Christians say a pastor should leave ministry if he uses porn

More than eight out of 10 youth pastors say they are very (28%) or somewhat (56%) well equipped to help teens who are struggling with porn. (Male, full-time leaders of groups larger than 50 students are most likely to say they are very well equipped. On the other hand, female, volunteer or part-time leaders with smaller groups feel less prepared.)

What We Are Doing for Pastors

Barna asked self-identified Christians 25 and older what they think should be done if a church finds out its pastor is using porn. Two out of five (41%) think the pastor should be fired or asked to resign. Three in 10 say he should take a leave of absence until he stops (29%). Combined, that's seven out of 10 Christians who say a pastor should leave ministry, at least for the time being, if he is found to be using porn.

WHAT SHOULD HAPPEN TO A PASTOR WHO IS FOUND TO BE USING PORN?

% among U.S. self-identified Christians 25 and older

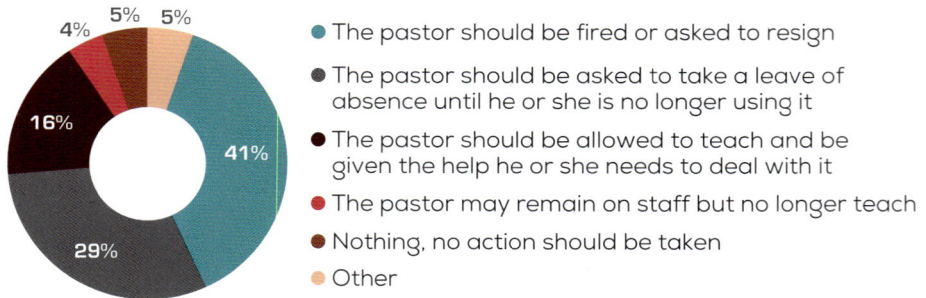

- 41% The pastor should be fired or asked to resign
- 29% The pastor should be asked to take a leave of absence until he or she is no longer using it
- 16% The pastor should be allowed to teach and be given the help he or she needs to deal with it
- 4% The pastor may remain on staff but no longer teach
- 5% Nothing, no action should be taken
- 5% Other

It may be that these are the right courses of action for a church, but it is also understandable, given these responses, why pastors might be inclined to hide their porn use at all costs. It is also important to acknowledge a serious—and unbiblical—double standard: One in five of those who say the pastor should resign (20%) and one in four who say he should take a leave of absence (27%) actively seek porn for themselves at least occasionally.

For their part, only 8 percent of pastors say a pastor struggling with porn should resign. Instead, he should find a professional counselor (82%) or a group of mature Christians who can hold him accountable (59%) and, if married, tell his spouse (58%).

WHAT MORE WE CAN DO (OR DO DIFFERENTLY)

Fifty years ago, writes researcher Mary Eberstadt,

> smoking was considered unremarkable in a moral sense, whereas pornography was widely considered disgusting and wrong—including even by people who consumed it. Today, as a general rule, just the reverse is true. Now it is pornography that is widely (though not universally) said to be value-free, whereas smoking is considered disgusting and wrong—including by many smokers.[90]

Just as with the example of smoking, there is hope that the cultural tide will shift and that the dangers and consequences of pornography will re-stigmatize both its consumption and production. But as long as porn continues to enjoy moral ambiguity, widespread acceptance and significant demand, its presence in and influence on our culture will expand.

For now, porn is everywhere and is likely to stay that way. It will continue to challenge and distort healthy expressions of sex, race, gender and relationships. The porn industry will, as it so often has, pry its way into more lives by adopting new technologies and further infiltrating the online spaces we inhabit.

Many pastors feel an accountability group is a good way to avoid porn use, yet many people resist being vulnerable about their sexual struggles. How can you, as a leader, model this kind of vulnerability in your own life? Who are you vulnerable with—how did you grow to trust that person?

CULTURE-WARRING "MORAL PANIC" HAS DONE ALMOST NOTHING TO CURB THE USE OF PORN

This presents a significant challenge to the Church. How do we respond to a crisis of such mammoth proportion? Historically, sex has been a major battleground on which the Church—in particular, the evangelical movement—has fought the war over culture. But just as we failed to reorient the moral shifts of the sexual revolution, we have thus far been unable to slow the swift change of moral sensibility regarding pornography. Culture-warring "moral panic" has done almost nothing to curb the use of porn or change people's perceptions of it.

Writing about the 2015 Supreme Court decision on same-sex marriage, Michael Gerson and Peter Wehner argue that Christians "require a new model of social engagement. . . . [Let's] take this moment to display the essential character of Christianity—one that appeals and persuades outside the faith."[91] They continue:

> If evangelicals are known primarily for defending . . . they will look like one aggrieved minority among many. The face of Christianity can't be the face of fear and resistance. Evangelicals will fail if they are defined by defending their own prerogatives. We should be known for, and distinguished by, a belief in the priority of humans—for defending their rights, well-being, and dignity.[92]

When it comes to pornography, we must come to terms with the cultural reality in which we find ourselves—not with "apocalyptic and hysterical rhetoric, characterized by white knuckles of fear and terror," but with "joy and grace, serenity and hope."[93] Christians have always lived, and even thrived, in cultures that do not reflect our values, particularly our sexual values. As in those times and places, Gerson and Wehner claim, "This moment can turn out to be not a calamity but a greater and grander stage for the true, enduring, and life-giving message of the gospel."[94]

We can keep the gospel as our first priority *and* counter the porn phenomenon by doing five things.

1. Reject the Morality of Self-Fulfillment

As we saw in chapter 3, the porn phenomenon can be understood as a result—not the cause—of a massive cultural reorientation toward self-fulfillment as the highest moral good. If this is so, then part of the Church's response must focus on rejecting the assumptions that underlie the new moral code, rather than fighting pornography as the ultimate enemy. As David Kinnaman and Gabe Lyons write in *Good Faith:*

> The extent to which the morality of self-fulfillment has taken hold of the hearts and minds of practicing Christians exposes an area of dangerous weakness in today's church. This grafting of cultural dogma onto Christian theology must stop. In order to for us to flourish as God's people, his moral order must be allowed to rule our lives.
>
> Living counter to the new morality is an uphill battle. Some days it feels like keeping the wind from blowing. Nearly everything about the broader culture is expertly marketed to appeal to our comfort, well-being, safety, and satisfaction. A delicious meal. Your dream holiday. The perfect house. Great sex. What will fulfill you?
>
> But then there is the way of Jesus.[95]

Some quarters of the Church are complicit in promoting the morality of self-fulfillment as somehow compatible with Christianity. It is not. And so long as Christians are willing to co-opt following Jesus in service to self-fulfillment, we cannot offer others an escape from the prison of their self-centeredness. "Our discipleship efforts must prophetically respond to the 'iSpirit' of

SO LONG AS CHRISTIANS ARE WILLING TO CO-OPT FOLLOWING JESUS IN SERVICE TO SELF-FULFILLMENT, WE CANNOT OFFER OTHERS AN ESCAPE FROM THE PRISON OF THEIR SELF-CENTEREDNESS

the age. We should lead people not only to convert to Jesus but also to de-convert from the religion of self."[96]

2. Rethink Our Approach to Sexual Ethics

We must also recognize our tendency toward disproportionate bias when it comes to sexual ethics. The biblical standards on sexuality are unambiguous, particularly for evangelicals and conservative Catholics and Orthodox Christians, but somewhere along the way the focus on sexual morality became somewhat single-minded. Gerson and Wehner claim, "Over the years, some Christian leaders have . . . succeeded in associating Christianity primarily with sexual morality."[97] C. S. Lewis, in *Mere Christianity*, offers a corrective:

> The sins of the flesh are bad, but they are the least bad of all sins. All the worst pleasures are purely spiritual: the pleasure of putting other people in the wrong, of bossing and patronizing and spoiling sport, and backbiting; the pleasure of power, of hatred. For there are two things inside me, competing with the human self which I must try to become. They are the Animal self, and the Diabolical self. The Diabolical self is the worse of the two. That is why a cold, self-righteous prig who goes regularly to church may be far nearer to hell than a prostitute. But, of course, it is better to be neither.[98]

THE BIBLICAL STANDARDS ON SEXUALITY ARE UNAMBIGUOUS, BUT SOMEWHERE ALONG THE WAY THE FOCUS ON SEXUALITY BECAME SINGLE-MINDED

This means treating pornography use in the Church just as we'd treat any other sin: with grace. Which leads us to the next step.

3. Create Communities of Grace

Balancing our approach to sexual ethics should, by consequence, lead to the creation of communities of grace. This means dispensing discipline that is proportionate and consistent with that of other sins. It means abandoning the shaming and condemnation reserved for those who struggle with porn. Sexual sin does not disqualify any pastor, lay leader, friend, husband, wife, brother or sister from the grace and forgiveness of God. The sex-positive camp has at least one thing right: Shame does little but drive sin into hiding, where it festers and grows in isolation from community and accountability. The Lord calls us to walk in the light, to confess our sins to fellow believers, but to do that we must create communities absent of shame and judgment, where our brothers and sisters can confess and repent of their sin and be met with love, acceptance and help to "go and sin no more."

> It's human nature to want to be wanted. It's normal for that desire to manifest in a desire for sex. The problem is that there is no good moral outlet for these natural desires before marriage, and our sex-laden society has done a wonderful job of causing most folks, men and women, to stir up and awaken love before it pleases. Being involved in a Christian community where it's safe to be struggling is essential. Every man I know who has achieved success in this struggle has been part of a strong accountability group where friends wrestle and pray over this together.[99]

Successfully waging a battle against porn use *can* be done in the loving company of a community of grace.

4. Present a Culturally Resonant Challenge to Pornography

The Christian community's challenge to porn must move beyond moralizing and shaming to sophisticated, critical engagement. We must remember that Scripture verses that command us to abstain from sexual immorality will win the day only among those who already agree with us. Our cultural engagement on the topic of porn must be offered in terms that can be understood by any person of goodwill—not just by a fellow Christian who shares our worldview.

SHAME DOES LITTLE BUT DRIVE SIN INTO HIDING, WHERE IT FESTERS AND GROWS IN ISOLATION FROM COMMUNITY AND ACCOUNTABILITY

Sex addicts choose a take-only relationship with a virtual lover over a give-and-take relationship with a real person. In doing so, they deprive their spouse of intimacy. The same is surely true of spiritual intimacy with God—and for a pastor this is especially concerning. How is it possible that a significant percentage of pastors believe their porn use does not affect their ministry? Could this misguided belief be a symptom of a deeper spiritual sickness of arrogance and pride?

Porn denies human dignity. Porn objectifies human bodies. Porn tells a false and inhumane story about people of color. Porn presents a picture of sex that is carnal, aggressive and often unrealistic. Porn is cruel, degrading and misogynistic, and distorts expectations of both masculinity and femininity. Porn destroys relationships, pathologizes sexuality and ruins the lives of children. The industry exploits and coerces actors, and by design or accident incites sex slavery and human trafficking.

Porn treats human beings as commodities.

5. Promote a Robust Biblical Counter-Narrative to Porn

In stark contrast to porn's lies, God's word says that human beings are created in God's image and thus are precious beyond compare. And sex is a God-created aspect of human life—it's not a dirty word.

Rather than treating it as such, we must celebrate and promote God's good intentions for sex as a counter-narrative to the false stories told by pornography. Church leaders must steer their congregations in more hopeful directions, away from the distorted picture of sex touted by porn, to a fuller and more biblical vision for sex. This means actually talking about sex and pornography, and contrasting God's plans with porn's lies early and often.

"Parents often remain reluctant to discuss sexual topics with their children, so today's youth are often left to their own devices to navigate the complex task of developing beliefs about sexuality."[100] Parents must provide a counterpoint to porn. Without it, "young people are going to find information wherever they can get it."[101] And information is not wisdom. Parents, church leaders and Christian mentors must acknowledge and engage with the reality of pornography if we are to provide young people with the critical tools they need to thrive in the porn-saturated world we inhabit— and we must offer a counter-narrative that makes sense of sex in the light of God's wisdom and goodness.

WE MUST OFFER A COUNTER-NARRATIVE THAT MAKES SENSE OF SEX IN THE LIGHT OF GOD'S WISDOM AND GOODNESS

▶ Q&A WITH MARLENE SOFFERA

Q: You co-lead a support group for wives of sex addicts. In your experience, what are the most common relational effects of porn use? What do you hear from women about the effects of their husband's sex addiction?

A: The breakdown of trust is the number-one issue reported by wives of sex addicts. This is true no matter the form in which their husband's addiction manifests itself, all the way from "simple" use of pornography to extramarital affairs (often with the wife's friends or relatives), prostitutes, rape, pedophilia, etc. Every one of these activities is shrouded in secrecy and layers of lies and broken promises. When the lies finally come to light, usually in a dramatic discovery, the wife's trust in her husband is almost completely shattered. It is a very long and difficult process to rebuild trust.

Second, a husband's addiction often creates huge self-esteem problems for his wife. A woman tends to compare herself unfavorably to the virtual women in her husband's life. She instinctively feels that she does not measure up. She is not enough in and of herself to satisfy her spouse, so her self-esteem takes a nosedive. On top of that, many a sex-addicted husband tells his wife about the many ways in which she is inadequate, actually blaming her for his addiction: "I wouldn't *need* pornography if only you . . . had bigger boobs / were thinner / wore your hair differently / were more aggressive sexually / were more passive sexually / wore this costume." The wife is left feeling worthless, guilty and shameful. Wives age, and simply cannot compete with enhanced pornographic females who are perpetually in their teens and early twenties.

MARLENE SOFFERA
Pastor, speaker, writer

Rev. Marlene Soffera is a minister ordained by the Church of God (Anderson). She has served local congregations as an associate pastor and as a lead pastor, and serves the wider church as a speaker at retreats and conferences. Marlene co-facilitates a weekly L.I.F.E. Ministries support group for wives of sex addicts, and leads workshops for clergy and lay leaders on the topic of pornography addiction. Marlene and her husband of 42 years, Greg, live in California.

A third damaging issue is a lack of intimacy, both emotionally and (often) physically. At its core, sexual addiction is an intimacy disorder. The addict often struggles to achieve a genuine emotional intimacy with his wife, often because of childhood wounds. He finds it much easier to bond with a virtual wife / sex partner because there is no need for relational give and take. There's just *take*. Perhaps surprisingly, sex addicts also often struggle with physical intimacy. A husband can't control the outcome of a sexual encounter with his wife in the same way he can when "engaging" just with himself. Many addicts deprive their wives of sexual encounters because: 1) They have difficulty achieving an erection or otherwise "performing" without the constant visual stimulation pornography provides, and 2) they have already "spent" themselves (sometimes several times a day) with their pornographic "partners." There is simply nothing left to give to their wives. Because of this emotional and physical distance, wives of sex addicts often feel very alone.

These three issues contribute to anger and depression in the wife, and often lead to separation and divorce. This goes on to affect generations of children and grandchildren. Pornography use and abuse is not a victimless crime. It is a crime against the whole family.

BECAUSE OF EMOTIONAL AND PHYSICAL DISTANCE, WIVES OF SEX ADDICTS OFTEN FEEL VERY ALONE

Q: Only about one in 11 churches has a program specifically designed to help people who are struggling with porn use. When about one-third of practicing Christian men and teen boys report seeking porn at least once a month, any ideas about why so few churches offer support within the worshiping community? What would you tell leaders who want to offer something but aren't sure where to start?

A: A number of Christian-based recovery groups for pornography / sex addicts are designed to be led by recovering addicts. They are not programs that "just anyone" can effectively lead. Church boards don't simply decide to start such a ministry like they might vote to start a food pantry or bus ministry. It's like Alcoholics Anonymous. It requires a leader to be transparent enough to say, "I'm a recovered sex addict, and I want to start a chapter affiliated with such-and-such ministry." That kind of vulnerability can come at a huge cost. Will the church leadership throw the guy off the board if he admits to that kind of sinful past or ongoing struggle? Will they "de-Christianize" him? If that man starts the group and promotes it to the congregation, will the laity shun him for his less-than-holy thoughts and actions? If that man is the pastor, will the church fire him for being a sex addict? Sex and sex addiction are a touchy subject in the church, shrouded in mystery, misunderstanding and a great deal of shame. Offering support within the worshiping community requires a very brave, committed and *recovering* leader who is willing to suffer negative consequences in order to provide healing and hope to others. Many congregations simply do not have a person who is sufficiently recovered to lead, or sufficiently brave to be that vulnerable.

If church leadership feels led to address the issue but doesn't have a qualified leader at hand, they can still find a path to ministry. That path begins with research. A simple Internet search for Christian sex addict recovery groups will yield several options to explore, such as L.I.F.E. Ministries, Covenant Eyes, etc. These groups have lots of resources, and can often direct people to a recovery group in their community or a nearby city. The pastor could inquire at the city's ministerial association to see if some other congregation already has such a support group in place. These groups are usually very willing to accept "outsiders" into their group. It is not unusual for one denomination to start and host a support group that ends up with participants from

SEX AND SEX ADDICTION ARE A TOUCHY SUBJECT IN THE CHURCH, SHROUDED IN MYSTERY, MISUNDERSTANDING AND A GREAT DEAL OF SHAME

"Youth ministry is ground zero for the porn phenomenon" because, as Rev. Marlene Soffera notes, "people choose how to deal with pain at a young age." Each younger generation is exposed earlier to porn because access to it is exponentially easier than ever. What can we do to educate and equip children's ministers, youth workers and parents— both on keeping kids from porn and on coaching kids to deal with pain in a spiritually healthy way?

many different denominations. Each separate church can promote and support the work of the church that started the ministry. (It's called *being the Church*!)

Q: Looking at the Barna findings, what (if anything) stands out to you as encouraging, and why? What (if anything) do you find discouraging, and why?

A: Encouraging: the fact that more and more people are approaching their pastor or youth pastor for help with their pornography issues.

Discouraging:
- Porn use is considered amoral or is increasingly accepted.
- A significant minority of respondents do not consider non-consensual sex acts to be "always wrong."
- Women's use of pornography is on the rise.

Increasing acceptance of pornography use will lead to increasing levels of actual sex addiction. Any, even slight, trend in the direction of normalizing non-consensual sex acts contributes to a worsening of our current rape culture. And women's increasing use of pornography will lead them into addiction just as it does for men, and the consequences will be equally devastating. The effects of a woman's addiction on her husband are just as devastating as a husband's addiction on his wife. All of the issues of trust, self-esteem, intimacy, anger, depression and so on are the same when the tables are turned.

Q: In your experience, how does life stage play a role in someone's motivations for porn use? How, if at all, does that change your approach to, say, teens and young adults from your approach to married, older adults?

A: The Barna research shows that people across the age spectrum use porn "for personal arousal" along with boredom, curiosity, fun, etc. The reality *for the addict*—differentiated from a more casual user—is that porn is their drug of choice to medicate the pain of past wounds (often these are "father wounds," and that's why I recommend therapy to get to the core of the problem). Few middle-aged people who don't already drink, do drugs or use pornography suddenly decide to start using. Rather, people usually choose how to deal with pain at a young age. While alcohol and drugs are most common, pornography is rising rapidly—and most young people do not even realize it is "medication." Curious teens or twentysomethings (or even children) are hooked long before they know the "why" of their woundedness. We need to address the issue with teenagers and point them in the direction of healing before that happens. Unfortunately, the challenge is how to do that with the awareness, full acceptance and consent of their parents.

For married, older adults, we're not dealing with new users, but people who have ingrained behaviors and corresponding issues. My approach is as I mentioned above: recovery groups, individual counseling and marriage counseling. It is extremely rare to hear of a miraculous prayer cure for an addict.

THE REALITY FOR THE ADDICT IS THAT PORN IS THEIR DRUG OF CHOICE TO MEDICATE THE PAIN OF PAST WOUNDS

▶ Q&A WITH RON DEHAAS

RON DEHAAS
President and founder of Covenant Eyes

Ron DeHaas invented Internet accountability in March 2000 when he founded Covenant Eyes, Inc. He has BS and MS degrees from The Ohio State University and is a PhD candidate at the University of Michigan. He lost his family in a car accident in 1992, and since then has been developing resources for the protection and betterment of families. Through Covenant Eyes' educational resources and Internet accountability software, he has directed over 1.5 million man-hours of battling pornography and sex trafficking. One hundred million Covenant Eyes Accountability Reports have generated 16 years of conversation-based accountability.

www.CovenantEyes.com

Q: Why did you start Covenant Eyes? What made you believe content-blocking software could not work as a sole solution to pornography use?

A: Internet filters don't work for most people over the age of 13. They are easy to circumvent and actually tempt people to get around them. And when they successfully circumvent the filter, nobody knows—so the user may be trapped by the predatory porn culture.

When I started Covenant Eyes 16 years ago, I had two teenage sons. Instead of legalistically blocking them, I wanted something that would start a conversation, an accountability record. A filter was fine for my seven-year-old daughter, but I wanted to train my sons in the disciplined use of the Internet. So I started Covenant Eyes Internet Accountability. We have a filter for those who need it, but accountability is the best.

The data from *The Porn Phenomenon* bears this out. Twenty-nine percent of general-population adults seek out pornography at least monthly. However, 39 percent of those who use a filter to block pornography seek it out at least monthly. More alarming, 54 percent of U.S. adults say they never seek out porn—*but 0 percent of filter-users* say they never seek it out!

That's why I started Covenant Eyes: Filters can't replace relationships for keeping people accountable.

Q: Do customers usually come to you to prevent pornography from becoming a problem or to curb an existing problem?

A: Both, but it's deeper than that. The majority of Covenant Eyes users are families—and every family has its own history and unique set of needs.

Many families have parents who do not use porn and don't want their kids to use it. Some have no children, but one or both spouses do use porn and are struggling to stop. Others who are struggling have kids and want both accountability for themselves and protection for their children.

The one thing they have in common is that they are "accountable families." Barna did a separate study on long-time (more than five years) Covenant Eyes users, comparing them to the data in *The Porn Phenomenon*. It's clear from the study of the general population that older generations have not been successful, for the most part, in passing on their values to the next generation.

However, Barna found that "accountable families"—those from the Covenant Eyes cohort— who take the spiritual formation of their family seriously *are* successful in passing their values on to the next generation.

Guess what? Good parenting works!

ACKNOWLEDGEMENTS

Special thanks to our generous Q&A contributors: Audrey Assad, Jefferson Bethke, Ron DeHaas, Joel Hesch, Robert Jenkins, Mark Regnerus, Marlene Soffera, and the National Center on Sexual Exploitation. Your insights help to make the data more human, reminding us that this research is about people and relationships.

Also to Pastor Bob Harper from the Ventura Vineyard, who contributed the ministry application questions offered throughout the monograph: Thank you for bringing these findings out of the realm of theory and into the lives of Christians trying to respond to momentous cultural change.

Researchers for *The Porn Phenomenon* were David Kinnaman, Joyce Chiu, Brooke Hempell, Roxanne Stone, Katie Fitzgerald and Inga Dahlstedt. Under the editorial and creative direction of Roxanne Stone, Joyce Chiu wrote primary analysis of the findings; Cory Maxwell-Coghlan contributed secondary research; Aly Hawkins edited the research monograph; Chaz Russo created the cover and infographics; and Rob Williams designed the charts, graphs and book layout.

METHODOLOGY

Barna conducted four online surveys in July and August 2015 for *The Porn Phenomenon* study, with a total sample of 2,771 participants. These quantitative studies were preceded by qualitative research in the form of an open-ended online survey with 32 adults and 20 pastors on the topics of pornography and sex addiction. This qualitative research served to inform the development of subsequent survey tools and to provide context for interpreting the findings in the final data.

The researchers felt that an online methodology was essential to ensure confidentiality / anonymity and candid responses, which would not be possible in a phone poll. Our team was still surprised, in the qualitative research, by the candidness of the respondents. Many related personal stories of their own or a family member's struggle, revealing the emotional factors surrounding pornography use.

The quantitative surveys consisted of parallel questions about perceptions of pornography, exposure, use and attitudes towards use. At the beginning of each survey, participants were warned of the sensitive nature of the questions and asked to confirm their interest in continuing. And again at the beginning of the section about pornography use, respondents were asked if they wished to continue due to the sensitive nature of the topic. *Only 3 percent of respondents dropped out of the survey at this point.* The total dropout rate for the entire survey was less than 40 percent (who initially started the survey, but discontinued at some point for a variety of possible reasons).

In a survey among U.S. teens and young adults, 813 participants between the ages of 13 and 24 were recruited and surveyed through a national consumer panel. The panel is representative by age, gender, region and socioeconomic grade, and no other screening criteria were applied. This survey included an extra module on "porn 2.0": the use of digital devices and social media for pornography consumption. Ninety-eight percent of teens and young adults continued the survey after the second sensitive topic warning. The sample error on this survey is plus or minus 3.4 percentage points at the 95-percent confidence level.

In a general U.S. population survey, 1,188 adults 25 years and older were separately recruited and surveyed through a national consumer panel. The panel is representative by age, gender, region and socioeconomic grade, and no other screening criteria were applied. This survey included an extra module on perceptions of pornography and the Church (for self-identified Christians who attend church regularly). These questions were parallel to those asked of pastors. Ninety-six percent of adults continued the survey after the second sensitive topic warning. The sample error on this survey is plus or minus 2.8 percentage points at the 95-percent confidence level.

In a survey of U.S. Protestant church leaders, 432 senior pastors and 338 youth pastors were recruited and surveyed through publically available Protestant church listings. These respondents were given a survey parallel to the main adult study, with an extra module for youth pastors of questions about "porn 2.0."

Senior pastor data was weighted to be nationally representative of churches by denomination, church size and region according to church characteristics from the most recent National Congregation Study by the Association of Statisticians of American Religious Bodies. Qualifiers for inclusion in the study were only that participant's role (not necessarily title) is that of senior pastor. Nearly all are in paid full-time roles (93%), 5 percent are part-time and paid, and 2 percent are unpaid volunteers.

Youth pastor data was weighted on denomination and region according to church characteristics from the most recent National Congregation Study by the Association of Statisticians of American Religious Bodies. Qualifiers for inclusion in the study were only that participant's role (not necessarily title) is that of youth pastor or leader. The majority is in paid full-time roles (71%), 19 percent are part-time and paid, and 10 percent are unpaid volunteers. An average of 95, and a median of 60, teens attend these pastors' junior and high school youth activities in a typical week.

The sample error for the senior pastor survey is plus or minus 4.7 percentage points at the 95-percent confidence level. The sample error for the youth pastor survey is plus or minus 5.2 percentage points at the 95-percent confidence level.

ENDNOTES

1. David Foxon, *Libertine Literature in England, 1660–1745* (Fort Lee, NJ: Lyle Stuart, 1965), p 45; see also H. Montgomery Hyde, *A History of Pornography* (London: Heinemann, 1969), p 14.
2. *Obscene Publications Act of 1857* (20 & 21 Vict. c.83).
3. Aee Eleanor Heartney, "Pornography," *Art Journal*, vol. 50, no. 4, Winter 1991, pp 16-19.
4. Miranda A. H. Horvath, Llian Alys, Kristina Massey, Afroditi Pina, Mia Scally and Joanna R. Adler, "Basically . . . Porn Is Everywhere: A Rapid Evidence Assessment on the Effects that Access and Exposure to Pornography has on Children and Young People," A Special Report of The Office of the Children's Commissioner, 2012.
5. Gail Dines, *Pornland: How Porn Has Hijacked Our Sexuality* (Boston, MA: Beacon Press, 2011); see also Julie Bindel, "The Truth About the Porn Industry," *The Guardian*, July 2, 2010. http://www.theguardian.com/lifeandstyle/2010/jul/02/gail-dines-pornography (accessed January 2016).
6. "A User's Manual," *The Economist,* September 26, 2015. http://www.economist.com/news/international/21666113-hard-core-abundant-and-free-what-online-pornography-doing-sexual-tastesand (accessed January 2016)
7. Rachel Bell, "James Deen Is Pissed Off About Racism in the Porn Industry," Vice.com, Sep. 3, 2015. https://broadly.vice.com/en_us/article/james-deen-is-pissed-off-about-racism-in-the-porn-industry (accessed January 2016).
8. Ibid.
9. Robert Jensen, PhD, "Is Pornography Immoral?" Gender Studies Lecture at St. John's University, February 4, 2013. https://www.youtube.com/watch?v=FyXcSXMbItE&feature=youtu.be (accessed January 2016).
10. Julie Ruvolo, "How Much of the Internet Is Actually for Porn?" *Forbes*, September 7, 2011. http://www.forbes.com/sites/julieruvolo/2011/09/07/how-much-of-the-internet-is-actually-for-porn/ (accessed January 2016).
11. "The Internet Porn 'Epidemic': By the Numbers," *The Week*, June 17, 2010. http://theweek.com/articles/493433/internet-porn-epidemic-by-numbers (accessed January 2016); see also Matt Essert, "14 Mind-Blowing Facts about Porn in America," Mic.com, January 10, 2014. http://mic.com/articles/78627/14-mind-blowing-facts-about-porn-in-america#.Q7EJfgTHh (accessed January 2016).
12. Holly Finn, "Online Pornography's Effects, and a New Way to Fight Them," *The Wall Street Journal*, May 3, 2013. http://www.wsj.com/articles/SB10001424127887323628004578456710204395042 (accessed January 2016).
13. "Pornography Statistics: Annual Report 2015," Covenant Eyes. http://www.covenanteyes.com/pornstats/ (accessed January 2016).
14. Eric W. Owens, Richard J. Behun, Jill C. Manning and Rory C. Reid, "The Impact of Internet Pornography on Adolescents," *Sexual Addiction & Compulsivity: The Journal of Treatment and Prevention*, vol. 19, issue 1-2, 2012, pp 99-122.
15. Ibid., p 100.
16. Johannes Grenzfurthner, Gunther Friesinger and Daniel Fabry, *Pornnovation: Pornography and Technological Innovation* (San Francisco: Re Search, 2008), p 49.
17. Ibid.
18. Ben Agger, *Oversharing: Presentations of Self in the Internet Age* (New York: Routledge, 2012).
19. Dennis Carlson and Donyell L. Roseboro, Eds., *The Sexuality Curriculum and Youth Culture* (New York: Peter Lang Publishing, Inc., 2011), p. 349.
20. Karen Peterson-Iyer, "Mobile Porn?: Teenage Sexting and Justice for Women," *Journal of the Society of Christian Ethics*, Fall/Winter 2013, Vol. 33, No. 2, pp. 93–110.
21. Ibid., p. 94.
22. Ibid., p. 93.
23. Carlson and Roseboro, *The Sexuality Curriculum*, p. 350.
24. Ibid.
25. Ibid., p. 355.
26. Peterson-Iyer, "Mobile Porn?"
27. Carlson and Roseboro, *The Sexuality Curriculum*, p. 350.
28. Bruce E. Drushel and Kathleen German, *The New Pornographers: New Media, Sexual Expression, and the Law* (New York: The Continuum International Publishing Group, 2011). http://www.academia.edu/510376/The_New_Pornographers_New_Media_Sexual_Expression_and_the_Law (accessed January 2016).

29. Ibid.

30. Carlson and Roseboro, *The Sexuality Curriculum*.

31. Peterson-Iyer, "Mobile Porn?" p. 100.

32. Lisa Myers, "The Pornification of Popular Culture: The Normalization of Sex Through Popular Music and Social Media," *Movable Type*. http://movabletypeuva.com/the-pornification-of-popular-culture/ (accessed January 2016).

33. Ibid.

34. David Kinnaman and Gabe Lyons, *Good Faith: Being a Christian When Society Thinks You're Irrelevant and Extreme* (Grand Rapids, MI: Baker Books, 2016).

35. Mireille Miller-Young, "Pornography Can Be Empowering to Women on Screen," *New York Times*, June 10, 2013. http://www.nytimes.com/roomfordebate/2012/11/11/does-pornography-deserve-its-bad-rap/pornography-can-be-empowering-to-women-on-screen (accessed January 2016).

36. Ibid.

37. Lilly O'Donnell, "Women in Porn: Empowering or Degrading?" Mic.com, November 19, 2012. http://mic.com/articles/19330/women-in-porn-empowering-or-degrading#.SpSIQsDps (accessed January 2016).

38. Helen Russell, "Porn Belongs in the Classroom, Says Danish Professor," *The Guardian*, March 15, 2015. http://www.theguardian.com/culture/2015/mar/16/pornography-belongs-classroom-professor-denmark (accessed January 2016).

39. Rhiannon Lucy Cosslett, "Sex Education Without Porn Is Not Sex Education," The Guardian, March 17, 2015. http://www.theguardian.com/commentisfree/2015/mar/17/porn-sex-education-consent-sexual-exploitation (accessed January 2016).

40. Markham Heid, "How Hot Women Help You De-Stress," *Men's Health*, July 10, 2013. http://www.menshealth.com/health/how-hot-women-help-you-de-stress (accessed January 2016).

41. David J. Ley, PhD, "Porn Is Not the Problem—You Are," *Psychology Today*, May 20, 2013. https://www.psychologytoday.com/blog/women-who-stray/201305/porn-is-not-the-problem-you-are (accessed January 2016).

42. "A User's Manual," *The Economist*.

43. Ibid.

44. Fabio D'Orlando, "The Demand for Pornography," *Journal of Happiness Studies*, March 2011, Vol. 12, Is. 1, pp. 51–75.

45. "Debate: Is Porn Always Degrading to Women?" *The Independent*, February 1, 2013. http://www.independent.co.uk/voices/debate/debate-is-porn-always-degrading-to-women-8477138.html (accessed January 2016).

46. Catherine A. MacKinnon, *Feminism Unmodified: Discourses on Life and Law* (Cambridge, MA: Harvard University Press, 1988), p. 176.

47. Paul J. Wright, "A National Prospective Study of Pornography Consumption and Gendered Attitudes Toward Womne," *Sexuality & Culture*, September 2015, Vol. 19, Is. 3, pp. 444–463.

48. "A User's Manual," *The Economist*.

49. Gail Dines, *Pornland*.

50. Ibid.

51. Dolf Zillman and Jennings Bryant, "Pornography and Sexual Callousness, and the Trivialization of Rape," *Journal of Communication*, December 1982, Vol. 32, Is. 4, pp. 10–21.

52. N.M. Malamuth and E. Donnerstein, "Pornography and Sexual Aggression," *Aggressive Behavior*, Vol. 12, Is. 3, pp. 225–228.

53. Caitlin Bancroft, "Porn Stars Can't Leave the Industry, and Here's Why," Mic.com, October 1, 2013. http://mic.com/articles/66025/porn-stars-can-t-leave-the-industry-and-here-s-why#.2tQONA1K0 (accessed January 2016).

54. Shared Hope International, *Demand: A Comparative Examination of Sex Tourism and Trafficking in Jamaica, Japan, the Netherlands, and the United States* (2007).

55. Freedom Youth Project, "Pornography: A Gateway to Human Trafficking," July 21, 2011. http://www.freedomyouthproject.org/2011/07/pornography-and-child-sex-trafficking.html (accessed January 2016).

56. Linda Smith and Cindy Coloma, *Renting Lacy: A Story of American's Prostituted Children* (Vancouver, WA: Shared Hope International, 2009).

57. "Child Pornography Statistics," Thorn Technology Taskforce. https://www.wearethorn.org/child-pornography-and-abuse-statistics/ (accessed January 2016).

58. Dines, *Pornland*.

59. Tracy Clary-Flory, "Pornography Has a Big Race Problem," *Business Insider*, September 1, 2015. http://www.businessinsider.com/pornography-has-a-big-race-problem-2015-9?IR=T (accessed January 2016).

60. Dines, *Pornland*.

61. Siobhan Fenton, "The Truth About Pornography's Race Problem," *The Independent*, September 2, 2015. http://www.independent.co.uk/news/world/americas/the-truth-about-pornographys-race-problem-10483042.html (accessed January 2016).

62. Donald L. Hilton Jr., MD, "Pornography Addiction: A Supranormal Stimulus Considered in the Context of Neuroplasticity," *Brain and Addiction*, Vol. 3, 2013.

63. DJ Mechelmans, et. al., "Enhanced Attentional Bias Towards Sexually Explicit Cues in Individuals with and Without Compulsive Sexual Behaviors," *PLoS One*, August 25, 2014. http://www.ncbi.nlm.nih.gov/pubmed/25153083 (accessed January 2016).

64. Simone Kuhn and Jürgen Gallinat, "Brain Structure and Functional Connectivity Associated with Porn Consumption," *JAMA Psychiatry*, 2014. http://archpsyc.jamanetwork.com/article.aspx?articleid=1874574 (accessed January 2016).

65. Norman Doidge, *The Brain That Changes Itself: Stories of Personal Triumph from the Frontiers of Brain Science* (New York: Viking, 2007).

66. "A User's Manual," *The Economist*.

67. Your Brain on Porn, "Porn-Induced Erectile Dysfunction," January 7, 2016. http://yourbrainonporn.com/erectile-dysfunction-and-porn (accessed January 2016).

68. Paulo Capogrosso, MD, et. al., "One Patient Out of Four with Newly Diagnosed Erectile Dysfunction Is a Young Man—Worrisome Picture from the Everyday Clinical Practice," *Journal of Sexual Medicine*, July 2013, Vol. 10, Is. 7, pp. 1833–1841.

69. Ivan Landripet, PhD, and Aleksandar Stulhofer, PhD, "Is Pornography Use Associated with Sexual Difficulties and Dysfunctions Among Younger Heterosexual Men?" *Journal of Sexual Medicine*, May 2015, Vol. 12, Is. 5, pp. 1136–1139; Nicole Prause, PhD, and James Pfaus, PhD, "Viewing Sexual Stimuli Associated with Greater Sexual Responsiveness, Not Erectile Dysfunction," *Sexual Medicine*, June 2015, Vol. 3, Is. 2, pp. 90–98.

70. Dolf Zillman and Jennings Bryant, "Porn's Impact on Sexual Satisfaction," *Journal of Applied Social Psychology*, April 1988, Vol. 18, Is. 5, pp. 438–453.

71. Victor Cline, "Pornography's Effects on Adults and Children," September 27, 2009. http://www.scribd.com/doc/20282510/Dr-Victor-Cline-Pornography-s-Effects-on-Adults-and-Children#scribd (accessed January 2016).

72. Pamela Paul, *Pornified: How Pornography Is Damaging Our Lives, Our Relationships, and Our Families* (New York: St. Martin's Griffin, 2006).

73. Paul J. Wright and Ashley K. Randall, "Pornography Exposure and Risky Sexual Behavior Among Adults Males in the United States," *Computers in Human Behavior*, July 2012, Vol. 28, Is. 4, pp. 1419–1416.

74. Zillman and Bryant, "Pornography and Sexual Callousness."

75. Joan Atwood, *The Effects of the Internet on Social Relationships: Therapeutic Considerations* (Bloomington, IN: iUniverse, 2011), pp. 165-166.

76. Ibid.

77. "Too Busy to Get Busy: Is Sexless Marriage on the Rise?" The Austin Institute, December 22, 2014. http://www.austin-institute.org/research/1526/ (accessed January 2016).

78. Cindy Gallop, "Make Love, Not Porn," TED, December 2, 2009. https://www.youtube.com/watch?v=FV8n_E_6Tpc (accessed January 2016).

79. "A User's Manual," *The Economist*.

80. Siobhan Rosen, "Dinner, Movie, and a Dirty Sanchez," *GQ*, January 27, 2012. http://www.gq.com/story/real-life-porn-sex-youporn-facial (accessed January 2016).

81. Catherine Steiner-Adair, *The Big Disconnect: Protecting Childhood and Family Relationships in the Digital Age* (New York: Harper, 2013).

82. Scot B. Boeringer, "Pornography and Sexual Aggression: Associations of Violent and Nonviolent Depictions with Rape and Rape Proclivity," *Deviant Behavior*, 1994, Vol. 15, Is. 3, pp. 289–304.

83. Mike Allen, et. al., "Pornography and Acceptance of Rape Myths," *Journal of Communication*, March 1995, Vol. 45, Is. 1, pp. 5–26.

84. Diana Russell, *Dangerous Relationships: Pornography, Misogyny and Rape* (Thousand Oaks, CA: SAGE Publications, 1998), p. 121.

85. Philipe Bensimon, "The Role of Pornography in Sexual Offending," *Sexual Addiction & Compulsivity: The Journal of Treatment & Prevention*, 2007, Vol. 14, Is. 2, pp. 95–117.

86. Robert Bauserman, "Sexual Aggression and Pornography: A Review of Correlational Research," *Basic and Applied Social Psychology*, 1996, Vol. 18, Is. 4, pp. 405–427.

87. Robert Jensen with Debbie Okrina, "Pornography and Sexual Violence," National Online Resource Center on Violence Against Women, July 2004. http://www.vawnet.org/sexual-violence/print-document.php?doc_id=418&find_type=web_desc_AR (accessed January 2016).

88. Ibid.

89. See *The State of Discipleship: A Barna Report Produced in Partnership with The Navigators* (Ventura, CA: Barna, 2015).

90. Mary Eberstadt, "Is Pornography the New Tobacco?" *Policy Review*, April / May 2009. http://www.hoover.org/research/pornography-new-tobacco (accessed February 2016).

91. Michael Gerson and Peter Wehner, "How Christians Can Flourish in a Same-Sex-Marriage World," *Christianity Today*, November 2, 2015. http://www.christianitytoday.com/ct/2015/november/how-christians-can-flourish-in-same-sex-marriage-world-cult.html?paging=off (accessed February 2016).

92. Ibid.

93. Ibid.

94. Ibid.

95. David Kinnaman and Gabe Lyons, *Good Faith: Being a Christians When Society Thinks You're Irrelevant and Extreme* (Grand Rapids, MI: Baker Books, 2016), pp. 60-61.

96. Ibid., p. 228.

97. Gerson and Wehner, "How Christians Can Flourish in a Same-Sex-Marriage World."

98. C. S. Lewis, *Mere Christianity* (New York: MacMillan Company, 1952).

99. Jordan Monge, "The Real Problem with Female Masturbation," *Her-meneutics*, April 2014. http://www.christianity-today.com/women/2014/april/real-problem-with-female-masturbation.html?paging=off (accessed February 2016).

100. Testimony of Jill C. Manning, C.S., "Hearing on Pornography's Impact on Marriage and the Family," to the Subcommittee on the Constitution, Civil Rights and Property Rights, Committee on the Judiciary, U.S. Senate, November 10, 2005, p. 26. http://s3.amazonaws.com/thf_media/2010/pdf/ManningTST.pdf (accessed February 2016).

101. Nisha Lilia Diu, "How Porn Is Rewiring Our Brains," *The Telegraph*, November 15, 2013. http://www.telegraph.co.uk/men/thinking-man/10441027/How-porn-is-rewiring-our-brains.html (accessed February 2016).

FACT SHEETS

ALL AMERICANS 13 AND OLDER

Top reasons for using porn:

1. Personal arousal (63%)
2. Curiosity (33%)
3. It's just fun (30%)
4. To get tips or ideas for my own sex life (29%)
5. Boredom (27%)

- One in five Americans uses porn weekly or more often (20%).

- One-third comes across porn weekly or more often, even if they're not seeking it (33%).

- Half say they never seek out porn (49%); one in six says they never come across it (17%).

- 17% of those who never seek out porn still come across it weekly or more often.

- Half consider viewing pornography wrong (50%).

- Half say porn is bad for society (50%).

- 78% of those who view porn use online videos; 43% use online pictures.

- 96% say porn involving children under the age of 12 is always wrong.

- 89% say depictions of non-consensual sex are wrong.

- 76% say porn involving teens is wrong.

- 69% say sexual images depicting someone in a demeaning way are wrong.

- 18% of porn users feel a sense of guilt about it.

- 68% of porn users are comfortable with how much they use.

- 4% of porn users say it sometimes hurts their relationships.

ALL MEN / BOYS 13 AND OLDER

Top reasons for using porn:

1. Personal arousal (66%)
2. It's just fun (34%)
3. Boredom (29%)
4. Curiosity (28%)
5. To get tips or ideas for my own sex life (25%)

- One in 10 American males views porn daily (11%).

- Half use it monthly or more often (51%).

- Seven in 10 use porn at least on occasion (69%).

- One in five comes across porn daily, even if they're not seeking it (20%); two-thirds come across porn at least monthly (66%).

- Three in 10 say they never seek out porn (31%); one in 10 never come across it (10%).

- Less than half consider viewing pornography wrong (44%).

- Eight out 10 of those who view porn use online videos (81%); half use online pictures (49%).

- 95% say porn involving children under the age of 12 is always wrong.

- 89% say depictions of non-consensual sex are wrong.

- 72% say porn involving teens is wrong.

- 66% say sexual images depicting someone in a demeaning way are wrong.

- Men are twice as likely as women to consider porn good for society (14% vs. 7%).

- More men (20%) than women (15%) feel a sense of guilt when they use porn and say they are currently trying to stop using it (11% vs. 5%).

- Two-thirds of porn users are comfortable with how much they use (68%).

- One in 20 porn users says it sometimes hurts their relationships (5%).

ALL WOMEN / GIRLS 13 AND OLDER

Top 5 reasons for viewing porn:

1. For personal arousal (57%)
2. Curiosity (43%)
3. To get tips or ideas for my own sex life (36%)
4. To set the mood with a significant other (33%)
5. Boredom (24%)

- One percent of American females use porn daily; 7 percent use it weekly.

- One in five comes across porn weekly or more often, even if they are not seeking it (21%).

- Two-thirds never seek out porn (67%, compared to 31% of males).

- One in four never comes across porn (23%).

- 55% consider viewing pornography wrong.

- Women are much more likely than men to consider porn bad for society (62% vs. 39%).

- 69% of those who view porn use online videos; 31% use online pictures.

- Among teens and young adults, 69% have received a nude image via text, email, social media or app (compared to 57% of males), and 51% have sent one (compared to 33% of males).

- 98% say porn involving children under the age of 12 is always wrong.

- 89% say depictions of non-consensual sex are wrong.

- 85% say porn involving teens is wrong, compared to 72% of men.

- 77% say sexual images depicting someone in a demeaning way are wrong.

- 15% of porn users feel a sense of guilt about it.

- 68% of porn users say they are comfortable with how much they use (the same as among males).

- 3% of porn users say it sometimes hurts their relationships.

ALL PRACTICING CHRISTIANS 13 AND OLDER

Top 5 reasons for viewing porn:

1. Personal arousal (45%)
2. Curiosity (30%)
3. To get tips or ideas for my own sex life (21%)
4. To se the mood with a significant other (19%)
5. Boredom (19%)

- 7% of practicing Christians view porn weekly or more often.

- One in four comes across porn weekly or more often, even when they are not seeking it (26%).

- 72% never actively seek out porn (compared to 39% of all others).

- One in five never come across porn (19%).

- Three in four consider viewing pornography wrong (73%).

- 77% think porn is bad for society (compared to 37% of all others).

- 69% of those who view porn use online videos; 36% use online pictures.

- 96% say porn involving children under the age of 12 is always wrong.

- 86% say depictions of non-consensual sex are wrong.

- 75% say porn involving teens is wrong.

- 74% say sexual images depicting someone in a demeaning way are wrong.

- Significantly more likely than all others to consider the following sexual acts to be always wrong: those that may be forced or painful (71% vs. 50%), that involve more than two people at once (43% vs. 12%) and between two people of the same gender (50% vs. 16%).

- Practicing Christians are more than twice as likely as all others to feel a sense of guilt when they use porn (34% vs. 15%) and to say they are currently trying to stop using porn (19% vs. 7%).

- Four in 10 porn users are comfortable with how much they use (39% compared to 73% of all others).

- 40% of porn users would rather not use at all (compared to 14% of all others).

- 7% of porn users say porn sometimes hurts their relationships.

ALL OTHERS*
13 AND OLDER

Top 5 reasons for viewing porn:

1. Personal arousal (67%)
2. Curiosity (33%)
3. It's just fun (33%)
4. To get tips or ideas for my own sex life (30%)
5. Boredom (29%)

- 8% view porn daily; another 17% view it weekly.

- 42% seek out porn at least once a month (compared to 13% of practicing Christians).

- 37% come across porn weekly or more often, even when they are not seeking it.

- Four in 10 never seek out porn (39%); 15% never come across porn.

- Four in 10 consider viewing pornography wrong (38%).

- Half consider porn to be neither good nor bad for society (49%, compared to 19% of practicing Christians); 37% say it is bad for society.

- 79% of those who view porn use online videos; 44% use online pictures.

- 96% say porn involving children under the age of 12 is always wrong.

- 89% say depictions of non-consensual sex are wrong.

- 75% say porn involving teens is wrong.

- 69% say sexual images depicting someone in a demeaning way are wrong.

- 15% of porn users feel a sense of guilt about it.

- Three in four porn users are comfortable with how much they use (73%).

- 4% of porn users say porn sometimes hurts their relationships.

*"All others" refers to all respondents who do not qualify as practicing Christians.

MARRIED ADULTS 25 AND OLDER

Top 5 reasons for viewing porn:

1. Personal arousal (54%)
2. To set the mood with a significant other (33%)
3. To get tips or ideas for my own sex life (32%)
4. Curiosity (28%)
5. It's just fun (23%)

- 3% seek out porn daily; another 9% do so weekly.

- Three in 10 come across porn weekly, even if they are not seeking it (29%).

- 61% never actively seek out porn (compared to 44% of single adults).

- 18% never come across porn.

- Six in 10 consider viewing pornography wrong (60%).

- 58% believe porn is bad for society (compared to 48% of single adults).

- Seven in 10 porn viewers use online videos (71%); two in five use online pictures (40%).

- 98% say porn involving children under the age of 12 is always wrong.

- 89% say depictions of non-consensual sex are wrong.

- 80% say porn involving teens is wrong.

- 69% say sexual images depicting someone in a demeaning way are wrong.

- 16% of porn users feel a sense of guilt about it.

- Six in 10 porn users are comfortable with how much they use (59%).

- 24% of those who actively seek out porn say they would rather not use porn at all (compared to 14% of single adults).

- Married adults are three times more likely than single adults to say porn sometimes hurts their relationships (6% vs. 2%) and that they are currently trying to stop using porn (10% vs. 3%).

SINGLE ADULTS 25 AND OLDER

Top 5 reasons for viewing porn:

1. Personal arousal (66%)
2. It's just fun (33%)
3. Curiosity (29%)
4. Boredom (25%)
5. Because it's less risky than actually having sex (22%)

- 7% of single adults seek out porn daily; 15% do so weekly.

- 37% actively seek out porn at least once a month (compared to 23% of married adults).

- One-third comes across porn weekly or more often, even if they are not seeking it (34%).

- 44% never actively seek out porn; 16% never come across porn.

- Less than half consider viewing pornography wrong (45%).

- Singles are twice as likely as married adults to consider porn good for society (13% vs. 6%); half consider it bad for society (48%).

- 71% of those who view porn use online videos; 34% use online pictures.

- 99% say porn involving children under the age of 12 is always wrong.

- 92% say depictions of non-consensual sex are wrong.

- 82% say porn involving teens is wrong.

- 72% say sexual images depicting someone in a demeaning way is wrong.

- 14% of porn users feel a sense of guilt about it.

- 74% of those who seek out porn are comfortable with how much they use (compared to 59% of married adults).

- Only 2% of porn users say it sometimes hurts their relationships.

- 42% say none of the people in their life know about their porn use (compared to 27% of married adults).

PRACTICING CHRISTIAN TEENS 13–17*

Top 5 reasons for viewing porn:

1. Curiosity (57%)
2. Personal arousal (43%)
3. Boredom (35%)
4. It's just fun (20%)
5. To get tips or ideas for my own sex life (13%)

- 6% of practicing Christian teens seek out porn daily; 12% do so weekly.

- 18% come across porn weekly or more often, even when they are not seeking it.

- 60% have never actively sought out porn; 25% have never come across it.

- 63% consider viewing pornography wrong.

- Practicing Christian teens are more than twice as likely as all other teens to say porn is bad for society (73% vs. 33%).

- 71% of those who view porn use online videos; half use online pictures (51%).

- 92% say porn involving children under the age of 12 is always wrong.

- 80% say depictions of non-consensual sex are wrong.

- 72% say sexual images depicting someone in a demeaning way are wrong.

- Half say porn involving teens is wrong (49%).

- Half of porn users feel a sense of guilt about it (53%).

- Three in 10 porn users are comfortable with how much they use (29%).

- 8% of porn users say porn sometimes hurts their relationships.

*Please note: The sample size of practicing Christian teens who report actively seeking out porn is small (n=26), so results from this study may not be nationally representative.

ALL OTHER TEENS
13–17

1. Personal arousal (71%)
2. Boredom (48%)
3. Curiosity (39%)
4. It's just fun (29%)
5. To get tips or ideas for my own sex life (28%)

- 9% of all other teens seek out porn daily; 20% do so weekly.

- One in three comes across porn weekly or more often, even if they are not seeking it (32%).

- Two in five never seek out porn (41%); one in five never comes across it (19%).

- One in three considers viewing pornography wrong (35%) and says it is bad for society (33%).

- 87% of those who view porn use online videos; 58% use online pictures.

- 88% say porn involving children under the age of 12 is always wrong.

- 85% say depictions of non-consensual sex are wrong.

- 72% say sexual images depicting someone in a demeaning way are wrong.

- 58% say porn involving teens is wrong.

- 27% of porn users feel a sense of guilt about it.

- 57% of porn users are comfortable with how much they use (compared to 71% of all other young adults ages 18 to 24).

- 2% of porn users say it sometimes hurts their relationships.

PRACTICING CHRISTIAN YOUNG ADULTS 18-24

Top 5 reasons for viewing porn:

1. Personal arousal (42%)
2. Curiosity (41%)
3. To get tips or ideas for my own sex life (35%)
4. It's just fun (32%)
5. To express my sexuality (29%)

- 9% of practicing Christian young adults seek out porn daily; 19% do so weekly.

- 44% come across porn weekly or more often, even if they are not seeking it.

- 46% never seek out porn (compared to 20% of all other young adults); 16% never come across it.

- Half consider viewing pornographic images wrong (51%).

- 63% consider porn bad for society.

- 16% consider porn good for society (compared to 3% of practicing Christian teens and 2% of practicing Christian adults 25 and older).

- 67% of those who view porn use online videos; 46% use online pictures.

- 29% mostly view pornography on their phone (compared to 11% of practicing Christian adults 25 and older).

- 77% say porn involving children under the age of 12 is always wrong.

- Seven in 10 say depictions of non-consensual sex are wrong (71%).

- 63% say sexual images depicting someone in a demeaning way are wrong.

- 63% say porn involving teens is wrong.

- Two in five porn users feel a sense of guilt about it (40%, compared to 19% of all other young adults).

- 46% are comfortable with how much porn they use (compared to 36% of practicing Christian adults 25 and older); equal proportions say they wish they used less (26%) or none at all (27%).

- One in five porn users say porn sometimes hurts their relationships (20%).

ALL OTHER YOUNG ADULTS 18–24

Top 5 reasons for viewing porn:

1. Personal arousal (70%)
2. Boredom (44%)
3. Curiosity (42%)
4. It's just fun (38%)
5. To get tips or ideas for my own sex life (36%)

- 12% of young adults who do not practice Christianity seek out porn daily; four in 10 do so weekly or more often (40%).

- 61% seek out porn at least once a month.

- 16% come across porn daily even when they are not seeking it; 32% come across it weekly.

- Three in four come across porn at least once a month (73%, compared to 51% of all other teens and 53% of all other adults 25 and older).

- One in five never seeks out porn (20%); 8% never come across it.

- 22% consider viewing pornography wrong (compared to 51% of practicing Christian young adults).

- Equal proportions consider porn good for society (23%) or bad for society (25%), with a majority saying it is neither (52%).

- 87% of those who view porn use online videos; 53% use online pictures.

- 36% mostly view pornography on their phone (compared to 12% of all other adults 25 and older).

- 17% mostly view porn through images sent via text (compared to 7% of all other teens and 2% of all other adults).

- 90% say porn involving children under the age of 12 is always wrong.

- 84% say depictions of non-consensual sex are wrong.

- Seven in 10 say porn involving teens is wrong (70%).

- 64% say sexual images depicting someone in a demeaning way are wrong.

- One in five porn users feels a sense of guilt about it (19%).

- Seven in 10 porn users are comfortable with how much they use (71%).

- 6% of porn users say porn sometimes hurts their relationships.

PRACTICING CHRISTIAN MILLENNIALS 25–30

Top 5 reasons for viewing porn:

1. Personal arousal (65%)
2. Because it's less risky than actually having sex (32%)
3. To set the mood with a significant other (31%)
4. Curiosity (26%)
5. Boredom (18%)

- 8% of practicing Christian Millennials seek out porn daily.

- One in three seek out porn monthly or more often (35%).

- 14% come across porn daily even when they are not seeking it; 30% come across it weekly.

- Half never seek out porn (51%); 8% never come across it.

- 81% consider viewing pornography wrong and say porn is bad for society.

- 76% of those who view porn use online videos; 35% use online pictures.

- 96% say porn involving children under the age of 12 is always wrong.

- 83% say depictions of non-consensual sex are wrong.

- Seven in 10 say porn involving teens is wrong (69%).

- 70% say sexual images depicting someone in a demeaning way are wrong.

- One-third of porn users feels a sense of guilt about it (32%, compared to 9% of all other Millennials 25 to 30).

- Half of porn users are comfortable with how much they use (49%).

- 17% of porn users say it sometimes hurts their relationships.

ALL OTHER MILLENNIALS 25–30

Top 5 reasons for viewing porn:

1. Personal arousal (71%)
2. To get tips or ideas for my own sex life (44%)
3. Curiosity (41%)
4. Boredom (38%)
5. It's just fun (34%)

- 8% of Millennials who do not practice Christianity seek out porn daily; 22% do so weekly.

- 14% come across porn daily even when they are not seeking it; 24% come across it weekly.

- 31% never seek out porn; 15% never come across it.

- Three in 10 consider viewing pornography wrong (30%, compared to 81% of practicing Christian Millennials).

- 38% say porn is bad for society.

- 80% of those who view porn use online videos; 41% use online pictures.

- All other Millennials are most likely to have started viewing porn before puberty (31% vs. 13% of all other Gen-Xers and 8% of all other Boomers).

- 94% say porn involving children under the age of 12 is always wrong.

- 87% say depictions of non-consensual sex are wrong.

- Eight in 10 say porn involving teens is wrong (81%).

- 67% say sexual images depicting someone in a demeaning way are wrong.

- Much more likely than all other Gen-Xers and Boomers to consider the following images okay: sexual acts that may be forced or painful (28% vs. 9% vs. 12%) and someone being depicted in a demeaning way (29% vs. 13% vs. 13%).

- One in 10 porn users feels a sense of guilt about it (9%).

- Seven in 10 porn users are comfortable with how much they use (72%).

PRACTICING CHRISTIAN GEN-XERS 31 – 50

1. Personal arousal (31%)
2. Curiosity (28%)
3. To get tips or ideas for my own sex life (28%)
4. To set the mood with a significant other (19%)
5. It's just fun & Boredom (18%)

- One in 10 practicing Christian Gen-Xers actively seek out porn weekly or more often (10%).

- 14% come across porn daily even when they are not seeking it; another 12% come across it weekly.

- Two-thirds never seek out porn (66%, compared to 27% of all other Gen-Xers); 17% never come across it.

- 72% consider viewing pornography wrong (compared to 33% of all other Gen-Xers); 75% say porn is bad for society.

- 73% of those who view porn use online videos; 22% use online pictures.

- 99% say porn involving children under the age of 12 is always wrong.

- 83% say depictions of non-consensual sex are wrong.

- 77% say porn involving teens is wrong.

- 74% say sexual images depicting someone in a demeaning way are wrong.

- Three in 10 porn users feel a sense of guilt about it (31%).

- 37% of porn users are comfortable with how much they use.

- 1% of porn users say it sometimes hurts their relationships.

ALL OTHER GEN-XERS AGE 31–50

- 9% of Gen-Xers who do not practice Christianity seek out porn daily; 19% do so weekly.

- 18% come across porn daily even when they are not seeking it; 24% come across it weekly.

- 27% never seek out porn; 12% never come across it.

- One-third considers viewing pornography wrong and says porn is bad for society (33%).

- 78% of those who view porn use online videos; 35% use online pictures.

- 99% say porn involving children under the age of 12 is always wrong.

- 94% say depictions of non-consensual sex are wrong.

- 77% say porn involving teens is wrong.

- 65% say sexual images depicting someone in a demeaning way are wrong.

- 13% of porn users feel a sense of guilt about it.

- Three in four porn users are comfortable with how much they use (74%).

- 6% of porn users say porn sometimes hurts their relationships (compared to 2% of all other Millennials and 1% of all other Boomers).

Top 5 reasons for viewing porn:

1. Personal arousal (67%)
2. To set the mood with a significant other (34%)
3. Curiosity (31%)
4. To get tips or ideas for my own sex life (31%)
5. It's just fun (30%)

PRACTICING CHRISTIAN BOOMERS 51–69

1. Personal arousal (50%)
2. Curiosity (25%)
3. Boredom (16%)
4. To set the mood with a significant other (15%)
5. To get tips or ideas for my own sex life (15%)

- One in 50 practicing Christian Boomers seek out porn weekly or more often (2%).

- 5% come across porn daily even when they are not seeking it; 19% come across it weekly.

- Eight in 10 never seek out porn (80%); 22% never come across it.

- 71% consider viewing pornography wrong.

- 76% say porn is bad for society.

- 47% of those who view porn use online videos; 38% use online pictures.

- 98% say porn involving children under the age of 12 is always wrong.

- 97% say depictions of non-consensual sex are wrong.

- 88% say sexual images depicting someone in a demeaning way are wrong.

- 85% say porn involving teens is wrong.

- Three in 10 porn users feel a sense of guilt about it (30%).

- 36% of porn users are comfortable with how much they use.

- Half of those who actively seek out porn say none of the people in their life knows about their porn use (51%).

- 3% of porn users say it sometimes hurts their relationships.

ALL OTHER BOOMERS 51–69

Top 5 reasons for viewing porn:

1. Personal arousal (54%)
2. It's just fun (33%)
3. Because it's less risky than actually having sex (22%)
4. Curiosity (20%)
5. Boredom (18%)

- 4% of Boomers who do not practice Christianity seek out porn daily; 11% do so weekly.

- 10% come across porn daily even when they are not seeking it; 16% come across it weekly.

- Six in 10 never seek out porn (61%); 20% never come across it.

- 53% consider viewing pornography wrong (compared to 33% of all other Gen-Xers and 30% of all other Millennials).

- 47% say porn is bad for society (compared to 33% of all other Gen-Xers and 38% of all other Millennials).

- 59% of those who view porn use online videos; 43% use online pictures.

- 97% say porn involving children under the age of 12 is always wrong.

- 88% say porn involving teens is wrong.

- 86% say depictions of non-consensual sex are wrong.

- 76% say sexual images depicting someone in a demeaning way are wrong.

- 12% of porn users feel a sense of guilt about it.

- 72% of porn users are comfortable with how much they use.

- 1% of porn users say it sometimes hurts their relationships.

YOUTH PASTORS

- 21% of youth pastors say using pornography is a current struggle.

- 43% say it has been a struggle in the past.

- 19 out of 20 have come across pornography, even if they did not respond to or engage with it (95%).

- 36% say they have never struggled with pornography.

- 99% say porn is bad for society; 92% say it's "very bad."

- 22% of current users view porn multiple times per week (compared to 15% of senior pastors who use porn).

- 56% believe they are addicted (compared to 33% of senior pastors who use porn).

- A majority of users views porn at least a few times per month (57%).

- A majority lives in constant fear of being discovered (56%).

- 94% of porn users feel a sense of guilt about it.

- 94% say they feel a great sense of shame about their pornography use.

- 41% say it sometimes hurts their relationships.

- 83% are currently trying to stop using porn; 68% have tried to stop but have been unable to (or started again).

SENIOR PASTORS

- 14% of senior pastors say using pornography is a current struggle.

- 43% say it has been a struggle in the past.

- 44% say they have never struggled with porn (compared to 36% of youth pastors)

- 93% have come across some type of pornography, even if they did not respond to or engage with it.

- 33% of current users believe they are addicted, 41% say they are not, and 27% are unsure

- A majority of those who currently use porn do so at least a few times a month (51%).

- 39% say the nature of their job makes it easier to use pornography secretly (compared to 19% of youth pastors).

- Senior pastors who use porn are less likely than youth pastors to feel a sense of guilt about their porn use (86% vs. 94%).

- 36% of current porn users say it sometimes hurts their relationships.

- Senior pastors are less likely than youth pastors to say they are currently trying to stop using porn (71% vs. 83%).

ABOUT

Barna Group is a research firm dedicated to providing actionable insights on faith and culture, with a particular focus on the Christian church. In its 30-year history, Barna has conducted more than one million interviews in the course of hundreds of studies, and has become a go-to source for organizations that want to better understand a complex and changing world from a faith perspective.

Barna's clients include a broad range of academic institutions, churches, non-profits, and businesses, such as Alpha, the Templeton Foundation, Pepperdine University, Fuller Seminary, the Bill and Melinda Gates Foundation, the Maclellan Foundation, DreamWorks Animation, Focus Features, Habitat for Humanity, the Navigators, NBC-Universal, the ONE Campaign, Paramount Pictures, the Salvation Army, Walden Media, Sony and World Vision.

The firm's studies are frequently quoted by major media outlets such as *The Economist*, BBC, CNN, *USA Today*, the *Wall Street Journal*, Fox News, Huffington Post, *The New York Times* and the *Los Angeles Times*. Visit us at barna.org.

Josh McDowell Ministry's mission is to serve others until the whole world hears about Jesus. As a ministry of Cru, JMM serves to help build multiplying disciples until the whole world knows that the Christian faith is reliable, relational and relevant to their lives. Josh McDowell Ministry equips students, parents, leaders and churches though the production of innovative events and cutting-edge ministry resources in the heart languages of people everywhere. Visit josh.org.

Covenant Eyes bridges the gap between technology and relationships through software that protects people on the Internet. Internet Accountability tracks websites visited on computers, smartphones and tablets, compiling them into an easy-to-read report using age-based content ratings. More than 100 million of these reports have started conversations that help develop family values and accountability. Internet Filtering blocks inappropriate web content based on age. Covenant Eyes serves over 200,000 members in more than 150 countries. www.covenanteyes.com